CW00540680

THE ART OF SELLING SONGS:
GRAPHICS FOR THE MUSIC BUSINESS
1690-1990

KEVIN EDGE

FUTURES PUBLICATIONS
LIMITED

FOR MY PARENTS

CONTENTS

The numbers of plates directly relevant to the text
appear in the left and right margins of the chapters.

Plates are supplied with the following information
subject to its availabilty at the time of going to press:
Object type; title or description; name and dates of designer (Des:);
illustrator (Illus:); photographer (Photo:); executor (eg engraver or
etcher, Ex:); technique; publisher (Pub:); printer (Pr:); date; size in
centimetres, height x width (sheet size is given unless otherwise stated).
All objects belonging to the V&A Museum are accompanied by their
accession numbers. For example: E. 55413–1919, 16409 and Circ. 492–1976.

ACKNOWLEDGEMENTS.

The opportunity of surveying music business graphics in the form of a Victoria & Albert Museum display was presented to me in 1988. It was offered jointly by John Murdoch, then Keeper of The Department of Designs, Prints and Drawings and by Susan Lambert, then Deputy Keeper and Prints Section Head. I am very grateful to them, both for the initial suggestion and for giving me their full support throughout the project's many phases.

This companion book grew out of work surrounding the selection and investigation of material for the display of the same name staged in V&A's Henry Cole Wing, February 20th to June 23rd 1991.

In writing the book I have inevitably relied on the scholarly writings of dozens of authors who have delved more thoroughly than myself into many of the individuals and subjects surveyed here. Without their efforts a synthesis of this nature could not have been written. Their names and publications appear in the References and Future Reading sections at the end of the book.

Everyone thanked here for their help in the preparation of this book are simultaneously thanked for their many and varied contributions to the display. The Museum is particularly grateful to those individuals, designers and companies who so willingly made gifts of music business material for inclusion in its permanent collection. Much of this has been selected for the gallery display and for reproduction on the pages that follow.

I would personally like to thank the following individuals and companies for so generously and patiently sharing their knowledge in response to my frequent requests for information and advice:

Ian Anderson and Nick Phillips of The Designers Republic, Lin Barkass at Opal Ltd., David Barlow, Ann Bradbeer of The Decca Record Company Ltd., Robert Carr, Carroll Dempsey & Thirkell, Dirk van Dooren, ECM Records in Munich, Fwa at Neville Brody's Studio, Kasper de Graaf and Assorted Images, Nigel Grierson, Graham Griffiths of New Note Distribution Ltd., Paul Khera; Andy Linehan, Paul Williams, Peter Copeland and library staff at The British Library National Sound Archive, Bob Linney, Barry Miles, Vaughan Oliver and Christopher Bigg, Jeremy Silver of The British Phonographic Industry, David Smart of Accident, Gee Vaucher, The Virgin Megastore Information Desk, Ivo Watts-Russell and 4AD, Brett Wickens and all at Peter Saville Associates. I particularly wish to thank Mike Dempsey, Malcolm Garrett and Russell Mills not only for all their help, but for allowing me to interview them and for granting permission for the reproduction of extracts in this book.

Thanks are due to the following colleagues of The V&A's Prints, Drawings and Paintings Collection for their encouragement, advice and help:

Stephen Astley, François Bardonnet, Joyce Baston, Catherine Bindman, Stephen Calloway, Shaun Cole, Lucy Davenport, Petra Gudlesheimer, Peggy Hughes, Mark Haworth-Booth, Lionel Lambourne, Alison Meyric-Hughes, Susan Jenkins, Ann-Louise Limm, Charles Newton, Ronald Parkinson, Sarah Postgate, Frances Rankin, Gill Saunders, Janet Skidmore, Raymond Smith, Michael Snodin, Moira Thunder, Margaret Timmers, Christopher Titterington, Peggy Vance, Rose Waight and Pat West. Special thanks are due to Adrian Craft for his unceasing hard work, enthusiasm and support. His sensitive eye proved to be invaluable in the selection and arrangement of the book's illustrated material.

In addition to giving me a great deal of advice and generous support, the following colleagues provided me with welcome editorial assistance at various times:

Malcolm Baker, Pauline Cockrill, Katherine Coombs, Rosemary Miles and Elizabeth Miller. My greatest debt in this regard is to Susan Lambert who patiently read several drafts and suggested improvements of many kinds.

I should also like to thank the following in other sections of the V&A for their contributions, great and small to this book:

Julia Bigham, Paul Greenhalgh; Nick Hindhaugh, Pauline Webber and their colleagues in Paper Conservation, Margaret Benton and colleagues at the Theatre Museum Covent Garden, Isobel Sinden and the staff of the Picture Library, Philip Spruyt de Bay, Stan Eost and their colleagues in the Photographic Studio, Meg Sweet of the Archive of Art and Design and Hilary Young.

I am grateful to my publisher Roger Loughney for giving his full support to the structure and scope of the book. I am also grateful to him for his willingness to tolerate the many additions made to the text over a period of several months.

Lastly I should like to thank:

Patrick Campbell, Tim Cargill, Richard Davis, James Firth, Paula Iley, Catherine McDermott, Sue and John Mold, Dr. Stephen Morris, Roger Sears, and Anthony White, for constructive criticisms, information and ideas on the subject of music and graphics shared in conversations of the past two years.

Kevin Edge, Kentish Town 1991.

INTRODUCTION

*Science, message and time – music is all of that
simultaneously. It is, by its very presence, a
mode of communication between man and his
environment, a mode of social expression, and
duration itself. It is therapeutic, purifying,
enveloping, liberating; it is rooted in a
comprehensive conception of knowledge about
the body, in a pursuit of exorcism through noise
and dance. But it is also past time to be
produced, heard and exchanged.*

Jacques Attali.
Noise. The Political Economy of Music
Manchester University Press,
English trans., 1985, p. 9.

INTRODUCTION

When 'good' music sings-out it sells itself and is consumed instantly by those who hear it. Music however, is a temporal, immaterial art, so that when musical voices and instruments cease to excite the air, it disappears. It leaves no visible trace, there is only silence.

Fortunately, those who like what they have heard can often repeat the pleasing aural experience and even 'hold on' to the music if replicas of it in the form of written transcripts, fresh performances and audio recordings are made available.

Those who earn a living by packaging and selling music as a product in this way must mark its presence with paper, explain what it is and convey its character through the use of printed graphics. Doing this makes the music palpable and visible, it is transformed into a static, material commodity that can be mass-produced, recreated, sold and owned for the mutual benefit of producers and consumers.[1]

Before the emergence of '...rapid circuits of electronic production/reproduction/distribution', paper and printed graphics were the sole means by which 'silenced' music could be packaged and sold.[2] In this age of radio, cinema, television and video, commercial products and messages are no longer carried and promoted by paper and ink alone, but it is only with these two, 'low-50' components that tangibility, content and stationary visual appeal can be given to the time-based, insubstantial product: sound ordered as music.

For frequent purchase and consumption of any commodified product to take place in a market, – be it a bottle of shampoo or a compact disc recording of Vivaldi's *Four Seasons* –

> ... people have to be informed [of] what products exist and where to acquire them. In other words, between manufacturers and consumers are the realms of distribution, marketing, advertising, mail order, shops and shopping.[3]

In this survey, the 'manufacturers' are professional composers and performers who supply music to 'consumers' who are amateur performers, audiences and individual listeners.

Between these two groups stands the music business. It is made up of '*realms of distribution*', run by marketing teams, advertisers and retailers engaged in the commercial mediation between composers and audiences involved in the musical activities, vocal and instrumental, private and public, which have flourished in Western culture since the end of the seventeenth century.[4]

It is the activities of these people and more importantly, the graphics generated by them, which are at the core of this survey.

The graphics they generate and use are defined here as intelligible marks, set down manually upon a surface by means of a pencil, pen, brush, knife, burin, etching needle, felt marker, piece of type, camera lens or computer terminal, to form letters and images that are reproduced in a variety of mechanical, photo-mechanical or photo-electric ways.

Materials and Method.

The approach taken in this survey is largely an inductive one, based on a thorough, first-hand examination of a large selection of modern and historical printed musical matter. Several trends have emerged, which have been interpreted in the light of the theoretical writings on music, design and cultural history now available.

Primary material studied includes title pages and frontispieces, choir-book pages, instrumental scores and tutor-books, broadside-ballads, songsters, posters, press advertisements, admission tickets, concert programmes, retail showcards, flyers, record catalogues, phonograph cylinder boxes, record sleeves, cassette, CD (compact disc) and DAT (digital audio tape) inlays. Many of these are to be seen today in national institutions such as The British Library as well as company archives, large and small. They can also be found in second-hand bookshops, record stores, antique shops, printed ephemera bazaars, in concert hall foyers, on the street and in the home. Much of the illustrated material comes from The Victoria & Albert Museum's Collection of Prints,

Drawings and Paintings, some examples being specially acquired for a 1991 exhibition of the same title. Secondary sources include discussions and interviews with fellow consumers and professional designers, the pages of the press and television and radio broadcasts.

The survey is divided into three chapters, one for each of the basic fields of commercial endeavour operating in the music business. Within each chapter, the graphic material found in the field under consideration is discussed in terms of form, production and use.

Chapter One looks at: *Lyric and score printing, distribution and sale.*

Chapter Two looks at: *The organisation and selling of music (live or recorded) as a regulated public performance.*

Chapter Three looks at: *Mass replication, distribution and sale of recorded sound.*

This particular ordering of the music business and its graphic output is intended to give the book some clearly defined shape in its sweep across some three hundred years of music selling in the West. It is rooted in a widely accepted understanding of the music business, underpinned with some theory inspired chiefly by a reading of Jacques Attali's socio-economic history of song-selling.[5]

Each of the survey's three chapters examines one part of commercial song-selling, giving prominence to the requirements, expectations, and aspirations of a small number of selected composers, performers, publishers, promoters, designers, printers, retailers and listeners. This is done in such a way as to give some impression of the complex conception, realisation and meaning of graphic forms past and present. Running alongside these examples is an account of a social history of music, selling practices, advances in printing methods, changes in taste and in technical modes of music consumption. The survey aims firstly to provide a broad historical-cum-material foil for students of contemporary music business graphics for whom there is very little written material that reaches back beyond 1967 and the appearance of the *Sgt. Pepper* LP. Secondly it aims to show that many current commercial practices, advertising formulae and graphic trends have a long historical pedigree stretching back to the age of Purcell.

Continuity and Change in the Art of Selling Music

A brief comparison between two, superficially very different printed examples will indicate some of the many continuities to be seen in this survey.

The first example, Bartolozzi's etching and stipple print of Handel after a drawing by Cipriani was commissioned as a collectible frontispiece-memorial by composer-turned music publisher Clementi for his c.1803–7 edition of Handel's songs. The second is the limited edition offset *1.8.a* lithography picture disc by photographer Jamie Morgan and designer Malcolm Garrett, produced for Virgin Records' 1983 release of Culture Club's LP *Colour by Numbers.* *3.24*

Both of these are 'extras' not found with 'standard' packages. Both are centred on compelling, well-loved 'star' musical personalities and both reflect the social imagery, fashions and music business perceptions of their respective periods. Even so, both go beyond any mere design formula to excite the eyes and rise above the visual clamour of the competition.[6]

They were both put together by revered graphic designers as compelling, virtuoso 'facades' for collections (a posthumous one in Handel's case), of songs by popular and successful composer-performers.[7]

Handel's portrait is a formal one of a be-wigged, deified creator, flanked by supportive musical and spiritual attributes; an image conceived by Bartolozzi's regular collaborator Cipriani, elicited by the publisher Clementi, and understood by the audience for Handel's music scored and sold in this way. The photo-portrait of Culture Club's Boy George shows a pensive, creative human being, framed by his musical colleagues and made-up to meet the expectations of Virgin Records and his fans.

Superficially different, one is black and white and the other colourful, both achieve their authority, relevance and style through their iconography, layout and apposite use of graphic devices.[8]

There is undoubtedly continuity in the conception, function and theme, if not in in the detailed form and production of music business graphics across the centuries. In essence, music's social and aesthetic roles have remained constant in respect of the consumer. This role has been nurtured and marketed from the very first by composers, performers, promoters, designers, publishers and retailers who have in general the same ambitions, skills, tactics and perceptions as their predecessors. All sought, and continue to seek to sell sound, influencing by graphic means, the perception and reception of the music, together with any associated ideological stance of relevance to the market, be it one of a punk group, 'authentic' chamber orchestra, baroque composer or 'new pop' vocalist.[9]

In the late 1980s, the music business and media in general, swiftly became atuned to the producer generated and consumer-fed preoccupations of retro-chic Acid-House with its 'smiley faces', flowers and 'day-glo' colours. The latter's fashionably 'postmodern', non-designed qualities were, before long, being marketed along conventional multi-media channels. In a creative, mainstream medium, where mass appeal is critical to the success of a new musical idiom, an independently-minded performer or a new graphic departure, their subsuming and packaging of that music by international commercial concerns, is unavoidable. This appropriation of a style's graphic essence also took-place with Psychedelia and Punk.[10]

As a result of these 'take-overs' and 'standardisations', the power of multi-national music corporations can sometimes be held to be over-bearing in respect of raw talent, yet the powers these companies do wield are so often ones of creation, support and promotion. They are therefore of direct benefit to consumers, and, as in earlier centuries, should, at their best regarded as patrons of the musical and graphic arts.

Graphics for the music business will of course, sometimes manipulate a compliant, innocent consumer and sway an indecisive record buyer faced with different versions of the same composition or several releases by the same singer. Other factors too, however, such as press reviews, cinema and television appearances, will also determine the reception and consumption of a new piece of music.[11]

In some instances, pictures and packaging possess an attraction for the buyer independent of the musical commodity they front. The potential autonomy of a graphic image is briefly discussed below.

Buying the Image: The Role of the Visual Aesthetic.

> The conceptual artist Cosimo scatters albums, with their plastic shrink-wraps still intact, around his apartment as sculpture. A colleague known as Collette makes montages of album covers and jewellery enshrined in plexiglass... the highest praise of album art is that it finally renders the record unnecessary, as a perfect idol displaces the god it represents.
> *Eisenberg, E. (1988) pp. 54-5.*

Although commercial graphics are, as a rule, not generated as unique works of art by an individual creator, but as functional visual devices fulfilling strict iconographic, notational, informational, or legal requirements, they do assume a degree of aesthetic autonomy subsisting as pictorial commodities of considerable appeal in their own right. This is not new; witness the pasting and pinning up of broadsides in the seventeenth and eighteenth centuries, the collection of colour lithograph song-sheets in the nineteenth century and the pinning-up of record sleeves and posters in the bedrooms of twentieth-century teenagers. The desire to collect these images is exploited today in the controversial ruse of issuing variant recording formats and accompanying packaging. The collecting impulse is a familiar and natural one, particularly in the realm of artistic confections. Eisenberg gives the following five reasons for the collection of music encapsulated on tape or disc:

i)   The need to make beauty and pleasures permanent.

ii) The need to comprehend beauty.

iii) The need to distinguish oneself as a consumer.

iv) The need to belong.

v)   The need to impress others, or oneself.

What must be asked is how many of these aims can be satisfied without the presence of universally comprehended iconographical, and informational graphic signs printed on the package?[12]

A new piece of music is often *seen* as a song-sheet, poster or record sleeve before it is *heard*. The immediately apprehended words and imagery in that case perform an informing, promissory, encapsulatory role, seeking to signify, by means of readily-understood visual terms, the likely idiom, origin, atmosphere, and qualitative nature of the music within. Once the music has been heard, the same words and images begin to operate as a specific mnemonic; a frozen visual analogy of the music which in some way conveys the aural, temporal nature of the represented piece to the mind of the consumer.

> I'm convinced that the sleeve design affects the way you hear the music. You see the record before you hear it...The music, the sleeve design, the way the band dress, all add-up together to mean something. It's not just an aural experience, it's an experience of meanings and connotations as well.
> *Kurt Ralske (Ultra Vivid Scene), Poynor, R. (1990).*

Exploration of the possible theoretical, spiritual, formal and actual (synaesthetic) relationship of hearing and seeing has been implicit and often explicit in the work of thinkers, architects, artists, and musicians from Pythagoras, Plato, St. Augustine, and Boethius through to Leonardo, Kandinsky, Klee, Cage, The Hafler Trio and Eno. However, beyond the geometric and numerical concordances existing between musical harmony and visual proportion, there seems to be no unmediated, universally recognised objective visual equivalent of music's pitch, timbre, or harmony as experienced by a human being.

As physical phenomena, light and sound do not interact in the general environment (though as Walker observes, they can, in some contexts be contiguous modes of expression), but enter our heads as two separate signals, they only become associated in the psychological, highly-subjective mental environment of an individual. Illustrators and graphic artists working in the music business seek to make visible with paper and print, their complex personal perceptions of light and sound. Using type and conventionalised imagery, they present the consumer, with an anticipatory visual symbol, and a subjective artistic interpretation of the invisible music.[13]

A parallel is to be seen in the history of musical instrument decoration where painted and embossed images, patterns and latin epigrams have served the same purpose as print has for saleable music, that is, to act as reflective or inspirational devices, partly stimulating the performer and establishing an overall mood of reception for the audience. This is particularly apparent with decorated keyboards and their cases in the sixteenth and seventeenth centuries which, even when silent, 'sang' of the wealth, leisure and learning of their merchant and courtly owners.[14]

Music is a succession of aural events occurring over minutes, hours or days. A static, two-dimensional image can never truly approach this auditory experience as it is a fixed expression apprehended in its totality within seconds. Only a lyric, printed score or narrative text can truly begin to offer the consumer a silent simulation of the music's temporal character.

> Music is still the highest thing in my life, and it frustrates me a lot because as in that old phrase '...all arts aspire to the condition of music...' in a piece of music you can sway a whole continent, you can influence people, you can make them depressed, you can make them happy, you can suggest colours...times in history...if you tried to paint all of that it would just be a mess. I've tried using nail varnishes which shift...and reflective paints underneath normal paints which just bounce light around...but that still relies on you having to be in front of the painting to experience those changes. In a piece of music you don't have to have that, it's going on around you, and its available to lots of people all at once.
> *Russell Mills in an interview with the author, 1989.*

The kinematic images of promotional films, television and videos are of course closer to music's projection across time. Many promotional videos operate upon a potential consumer at a subliminal level in that they masquerade and even function primarily as entertaining diversions. They indirectly inform the viewer of the presence of a new release and establish a performer's identity, but they do not impart important details of title, release date and catalogue number unless later added by retailers as the videos are shown on their in-store screens. Videos are thus subsidiary to the more significant role of static graphics and typography seen today on posters and record sleeves. Such graphics must be strong enough to survive translation and adaptation into any manner of sizes, colours and situations from small, black and white press advertisements through to large, multi-coloured stage sets.

2.10.b

Subsidiary music business graphics of today such as those seen on television shows, in television advertisements and on merchandise like t-shirts, caps, stickers and badges are, like video 'promos', not given any sustained consideration in this book. They may themselves elicit support from paper and ink but the graphics seen are nearly always of commercial necessity borrowings or reflections of determinant forms which are generated close to the over-arching commodity, namely the recording package.

Now that home-taping and cheaper illegal alternatives abound, it is vital for the business to recognise, cultivate and project the qualities of usefulness and aesthetic appeal into the packaging and marketing of music, and at the same time, remain attuned to shifting consumer preoccupations and aspirations. In the successful reaches of the music business there has been, and will continue to be this cultural-commercial dialogue mediated by graphic artists, typographers and photographers.[15]

Notes:

1   For a lucid and sustained socio-economic account of the commodification of song see Attali, J. (1985) pp. 12–8 & 36–9. Attali sees the *'immateriality of the commodity...'* result, at the advent of printing in *'...the exchange of pure signs...'*, music *'could be stockpiled, the sign was already for sale.'* ibid. p.53. For a more discursive account of the 'reification' of music see Eisenberg, E. (1988) pp. 9–28. On the production of non-material cultural goods see Hirsch, P. M. (1972). On promotion, product design, packaging, pricing and distribution as key aspects of successful selling and marketing see Sinclair, J. (1987) p. 4 et seq. & p. 93.

2   Chambers, I. (1988) p. 185.

3   Walker, J. A. (1989) pp. 175–6.

4   The business encompasses various operations geared to the encouragement, performance and subsequent encapsulation for sale, of live or recorded music, for financial gain. It therefore includes concert, music hall and night club owners, recording studios, music promoters, publishers, record companies, designers, printers, and retailers. For an interesting account of independent concert promoters see Darling, A. and Glanvill, R. (1989). Allied to, but distinct from the above, are radio and dance DJs, film and video-makers, television and press journalists, musical instrument and audio equipment manufactures. The need to distinguish 'pop' from 'serious', 'rock' from 'classical' or even instrumental from vocal has been kept to a minimum in this survey as the underlying constraints of music's social role, and the production, marketing and packaging of that music for consumption using paper and ink override such shifting, subjective classifications. For discussions of such terms see Cutler, C. (1985) and Middleton, R. (1990) pp. 3–7.

5   Attali, J. (1985) For Attali, music as a ritual and social necessity has in the past three hundred years been broken-down and packaged, managed and sold to the solitary and pacified consumer. This, Attali maintains is a result of a specialisation of its practice by professional performers with printed scores, the sale of it as a concert spectacle, and then its disembodiment and stockpiling as recordings.

6   See Attali, J. (1985) pp. 68–77 on the 'genealogy of the star', and Frith, S. (1990) on personality, image and consumption in '80s pop.

7   It is common in the music business to employ the best artists, designers and illustrators of the day to generate graphics with the requisite powers of communication. Witness the business employing the talents of Gravelot, Cruikshank and Concanen through to Picasso, Warhol and Brody.

8   These two examples are simple portrait types modified by social preoccupations, technical limitations and music business strictures which are to be seen throughout the three centuries in question. Some other basic departure points used with equal frequency in all aspects of the business throughout the period are annexed reproductions of fine art imagery and recycled popular musical imagery used as intimations of aesthetic and qualitative affinities or cultural pedigree. See Walker, J. A. (1987) pp. 87–94 and Carr, R., Case, B. and Dellar, F. (1986) pp. 128–139. Just as musical 'quotations' are often used to flatter a knowing audience, visual 'quotations' are used to flatter a knowing viewer. Recurrent thematic motifs in print tend to be pastoral scenes, romantic scenes, relaxing performers or performers in full musical flight, fantastic confections, ethnic or subcultural symbols.

9   On the centrality of music in society's rituals see Eisenberg, E. (1988) pp. 21–2.

10 On postmodernism and pop music see Frith, S. and Horne, H. (1987) pp. 3–8 and Readhead, S. (1990) pp. 1–26. See Readhead generally for accounts of the commercial confections and overall dynamics of the music business based on its own history and the youthful, less systematised musical and cultural margins. *'The advertisement does not so much invent social values or ideals of its own as it borrows, usurps, or exploits what advertisers take to be prevailing social values':* M.Schudson cited Sinclair, J. (1987) p. 29. Sinclair also sounds a note of caution: *'The image or cultural position which an advertisement assigns to a certain product may be attractive to people who never buy the product. Conversely they may buy products without being aware or caring about the images they carry.'* ibid. p. 63. Buxton argues that the record business sees the record as

having no precise use value and therefore has an infinite capacity to absorb signifiers which can be designed to create responses in the maximum number of potential consumers, Buxton, D. (1983). On the influence of independent label picture sleeve iconography in the late 1970s on mainstream packaging see Wozencroft, J. (1988) p. 52.

11 On hype in the music business see Grant, S. *et al*, (1989) and Smith, G. (1989).

12 Eisenberg, E. (1988) pp. 14–16.

13 Walker, J. A. (1987) p. 6. The Hafler Trio have experimented with the direct application of sound waves onto surfaces capable of registering patterns inherent in these waves. See The Hafler Trio (1986).

14 See Rueger, C. (1986).

15 For an interesting analysis of the mass media which facilitate (or perhaps hinder) such a dialogue see Walker. J. A. (1983) pp. 18–9.

SELLING THE LYRIC,
SELLING THE DOTS

BROADSIDES, SONG-SHEETS AND MUSIC-BOOKS

*'If ther be any jarre or dissonance, blame not
the printer who...doth heere deliver to thee a
perfect and true coppie...*

An extract from the preface of William Byrd's 1588
Collection: *Psalmes, Sonnets & Songs*
Cited Wulstan, D. (1985) p. 172.

SELLING THE LYRIC, SELLING THE DOTS
BROADSIDES, SONG-SHEETS AND MUSIC-BOOKS

Printed Lyrics, Musical Notes and Title Pages: Their Function and Form.

The printed lyric and musical notation (the 'dots') of a song relay performance directions to singers and instrumentalists. This process of sight-reading results in the time-based recreation of a piece of music, rather as a play's text when read and acted-out recreates events and narrative in time.[1]

Melodies and lyrics do not need to be commercially printed to enable them to be communicated. They can be passed directly from one composer or musician to another in manuscript form or by practical demonstration. Exposure to live and recorded music also expands a musician's repertoire without recourse to any printed score.[2] Simple agreement to play over a predetermined chord sequence as in jazz or rock, within the pre-selected rhythmic structure or *compás* of flamenco or to extemporize over a predetermined number of bars, as directed by a composer in a concerto cadenza, is sufficient to generate a good deal of music.[3] Popular compositions can appear in abbreviated forms in the pages of so-called 'fake-books', short-circuiting the attentions of designers and self-conscious publishers to serve as prosaic working documents with no pretence to beauty or decoration. Their value lies only in their authenticity to the original conception and are today frequently encountered as workaday photocopies circulating amongst musicians.

When a decision is taken to distribute and visually enliven a composition as a printed lyric and score to be performed without assistance from the composer, a lot of attention is paid to the quality of the printed words and 'dots'. To begin with, the lyric must be easy-to-read, accurate and attractive. This depends on the skillful choice of type-face or calligraphic style of engraving, and on the co-ordination of type and restrained use of complementary graphic motifs such as headpieces, rules and fleurons. Words on the sheet must be clear, unified arrangements of letters, easy on the eye, laid out in such a way as to reflect the metre of the verses. What has proved to be much more demanding has been the search for printed musical notation that succinctly and accurately conveys the details of a composition's harmonic and temporal structure, melody and phrasing. This search has extended beyond typographers and printers to include the efforts of composers (many of them well-known) who have devised their own type-faces, engraved or lithographed their own scores or who have generally paid some attention to the visual appeal of a work.[4]

In front of the lyric and the 'dots' designed to serve the professional and amateur musician stand the title pages. These are secondary elements in a musical publication which in a sense serve as graphic 'packaging' to mark the presence of a work and promote the identity of associated persons and products. They offer designers a greater opportunity for graphic invention and elaboration, being separate 'extras' and as such are frequently florid and expressive in character, establishing a visual encapsulation of the piece and imparting a significant visual aesthetic which will probably have a positive effect on any musicians and non-musicians during the selection of a particular edition.[5]

In addition to proclaiming the name of a piece, title pages often carry information concerning composer, arranger, lyricist, and references to other works by the same. Title page copy will also announce the success of the piece in performance or on record, list copyright details and give typographer, designer, printer and publisher credits. Other arrangements of the same piece or other works in the same series may also be advertised on the title page as might price lists of pieces by different composers available from the same publisher.

Close inspection of printed lyrics and scores reveals that there is a tremendous qualitative range in the layout and execution of a musical publication. Many lyrics and scores are prosaic, cheaply (and frequently illegally) produced objects printed on inferior paper with worn or out-moded blocks and plates, printed only with a view to achieve rapid, high-volume sales. This variation in quality evident, not only in pirated copies of many works across the centuries but in legitimate editions where insubstantial etching, imitation engraving (échoppe and etching), or lithography masquerade as more highly regarded, burin-work.

The Business of Music Before 1690

The Middle Ages. Prior to the advent of commercial printing on paper in fifteenth-century Europe, lyrics and music were, where necessary, circulated in manuscript on parchment.

In the realm of sacred music, texts sung at Divine Offices or at Mass were produced in scriptoria for use in choir as unique, large format codices and as master copies enshrining important settings. The precise nature of the production of these sacred musical works is still open to conjecture. What is likely is that most would have been commissioned by a religious or secular patron being copied from an exemplar and decorated either by an established scriptorium or by itinerant scribes and illuminators. New compositions and settings would have been passed to scribes on parchment-equivalents of the sixteenth century *cartelle*: prepared sheets ruled with a stave over which the polyphonic composition and text would be temporarily inscribed.

Service-books, being in essence transmitters of the word of God, were highly revered sacred artifacts, taking their place alongside the chalice and the Gospels. As a consequence, they were highly decorated with illuminated initials, incipits and ostentatious bindings.

The scriptoria had to strike a balance between the prestigious nature of the work which called for fine ornamentation and the practical, musical requirements of the performers. Formal appearances in these cases invariably owed as much to *1.16* precedent and tradition as to fresh endeavour.

Monies may have underlain commissions but it is most likely that reciprocity agreements would have been drawn up so that a manuscript might be produced in a simple exchange for building material or grants of land.

Financial exchange certainly surrounded the production of illuminated psalters for private lay devotion in cities like Paris which, by the mid-thirteenth century had become a centre for the secular commercial production of musical and literary works of all kinds used by the court, religious houses and university.

The Bodleian Library possesses an Oxford writing master's parchment poster from the early fourteenth century which today survives as four fragments of discontinuous text and music. It presumably served as a general advertisement or samples-sheet from which service books in a variety of styles (at different prices?) could be ordered. [6]

Surviving profane lyrics and settings are much in evidence in historic libraries and attest the healthy interweaving of sacred and secular music-making at court, in the cloister, in church and in the village in the Middle Ages as courtiers, pilgrims, soldiers and labourers traversed Europe. Formal evidence seen in surviving 'Saints' Lives' of the period suggests that single-leaf manuscripts of popular profane lyrics (and less likely music) transcended the aural transmission networks, to circulate in a form not dissimilar to the printed broadside-ballads of later centuries, with pictorial headpieces and columns of text promoted by singing ballad-mongers.

The introduction of printing from moveable type and woodblocks in the 1450s did not have any immediate effect on the production and dissemination of musical notation. Problems of legibility, underlay (the matching of words with notes), and visual appeal were considerable, and in any case, demands for a particular musical setting would have little commercial potential, often being confined to the finite market of a single diocese. The slow evolution from pen to press is graphically illustrated in the so-called *Constance Gradual* of c.1473, the earliest datable example of printed music, where illuminated initials share pages with moveable-type notation. Woodcut-broadsides, that is printed texts taken from simple relief-blocks devoid of any notation, were relatively easy to produce and were distributed at fairs and markets. Pilgrimage centres exploited the new technology of printing to bolster their long-established businesses of selling mementoes to pilgrims by producing such attractive relief-block broadside lyrics.[7]

European Developments in the Sixteenth and Seventeenth Centuries. By the sixteenth century, musical activity in all urban areas of Europe had become so pronounced that many professional composers sought to lay claims to parts of a nascent printing and publishing business, seeing it as a route to career advancement and profit. In Tudor England, John Rastell (c.1475–1536) is credited with two 'firsts' in the business of music printing: the first broadside to carry notation and, with his *Tyme to Pass with Goodly Sport* (c.1525), the world's first printing of a full score.

In the 1520s, English merchant stationers were granted the general right to duplicate works. This encouraged members of the select Stationers' Company to print and publish all manner of music in relatively attractive and sophisticated forms. The task of printing of gothic-type 'black-letter' street ballads free of musical notation remained with those inferior printers only allowed to print on one side of a sheet. These latter were the forerunners of broadside-ballad printers like Catnach, discussed below, operating on the printing-publishing fringe some three hundred years later.

Tudor composers William Byrd (1543–1623) and Thomas Tallis (c.1505–85), asserted their renown as servants of the court by obtaining a music-printing monopoly, details of which were published for all to see in their *Cantiones Sacrae* of 1575. It gave them and their associates the right to oversee the printing of songs and instrumental pieces from any source, British or Continental, for church or for chamber, together with the all-important monopolistic right to sell ruled (i.e. staved) paper.[8]

Professional performers at this date (and in fact well into the eighteenth century) were still most likely to study new work from manuscript sheets provided by copyists who extracted parts from full scores set down by composers. Until the introduction of improved intaglio techniques of music printing at the end of the seventeenth century, publication of music at all levels, popular and learned, was largely confined to short runs of sacred editions or private commissions where patrons would be certain to appreciate the eloquently engraved lines comparable to conti-

1.2.a nental practices and taste.[9]

At the amateur level at this date, and even more so in the following centuries, cheap, plentiful copies in print of the latest tunes and topical lyrics unfailingly scanning well-loved melodies were much in demand. Together with some 'luxury' editions, conceived as refined commodities in an emerging luxury goods market, they were the best route to profit for those then in the music business.

During the Commonwealth and Protectorate in England (1649–53) there was little demand for high church and professional courtly music. Music-making centred on the home and gave rise to the demand for large numbers of elegant, well-printed, easy-to-play pieces of music for middle-class domestic consumption. Slowly these conditions fostered what were to become the origins of the modern music business.

The 'Industry' of John Playford. In the mid-seventeenth century John Playford (active 1623–86), pointed the way for energetic commercialism in music publishing. Initially an amateur musician and composer, he sought to stimulate a market for his music by publishing musical tutor-books. It is calculated that he instigated the publication of some one hundred music-titles. His success is attributable to two factors: quality control and energetic retailing.[10] He closely supervised all stages of publication, displaying considerable knowledge of what would be acceptable to an increasingly discriminating consumer faced with a growing selection of high and low musical diversions. In his *Select Ayres and dialogues* of 1659 Playford described himself as '...*dayly attending the oversight of the presse...*' to ensure accuracy for '...*Publick Benefit and the Author's Reputation...*'[11] Copy on the title page of the successful John Hilton Junior (1599–1657) anthology *Catch that Catch Can*, printed for Playford and his master John Benson in London in 1652, proclaims two points of sale: St. Dunstan's Church Yard and the Inner Temple near the Church door. Proving to be a successful formula, this anthology of catches, rounds and canons was reissued in the late 1650s and again in the following decade. Playford himself added to the genre with his *Musical Companion*, first printed in 1673.

He cleverly exploited the status of the composer Henry Purcell (1659–95) on the title page of his *Sonnata's of III Parts* (sic.), published in 1683 by emphasising his exalted position as composer and organist to Charles II. To attract the refined, *1.2.c* tutored consumer and develop profitable sales at the luxury end of the market, music publishers emphasised the inherent differences between street-song and instrumental chamber music. In the preface there is an explanation of the objectives of the publication:

> Just imitation of the most famed Italian masters; principally, to bring the seriousness and gravity of that sort of Musick into vogue and reputation

among our countrymen whose humour, 'tis time now, should begin to loath the levity and balladry of our neighbours.[12]

Playford was imitated in his great pitches at the new musical markets by other London publishers such as Thomas Cross Junior (1660?–65) and John Walsh (c.1665–1736). The latter's career encompassed the issue of broadsides and frequent issues of stage song anthologies which gained immediate approval from London audiences, theatre owners and performers alike. His success in this field won him the prestigious task of publishing the work of Handel.

Some insight into the seventeenth-century practices of 'selling music' can be discerned in the words and actions of Shakespeare's roguish peddler Autolycus in *The Winter's Tale* (1611) and in the activities of the ballad-monger Nightingale in Ben Jonson's play *Batholomew Fayre* (1614). At this date, and for years to come, ballad-mongers would instill desire in the ears of a possible buyer simply by singing freshly penned and printed lyrics (free of notation) to well-known or catchy new tunes. The following dramatic extract from *Bartholomew Fayre,* act III, scene V, vividly shows the contempt many cared to show for the quality and origin of ballads sold on the streets.

Cokes' sister, Mrs Overdo asks him about the broadsides being proffered by the ballad-monger Nightingale: *'Has't a fine picture brother?',* Cokes replies, partly to his sister and partly to Nightingale:

> O sister do you remember the ballads over the nursery chimney at home of your own pasting-up? There be brave pictures. Other manner of pictures than these friend.

Later, after hearing one of Nightingale's new songs, Johnson's ridiculed bourgeoisie, Cokes tells another fayre-goer to get behind him in the queue for ballad slips and says he wishes to *'...buy the whole bundle...'*

It is interesting to note that Jonson's portrayal of Nightingale as an isolated figure selling sheets to a society branding him as a quick-witted though ultimately despicable character, is one which persists until the end of the nineteenth century, bolstered by the contempt of establishment commerce. The actual practices of selling, singing from and pasting or pinning-up ballads, is to be seen in many Dutch genre etchings of the seventeenth century, and also at a later date in engravings by William Hogarth (1697–1764).[13]

Printing and Selling Music in England, c.1690–c.1790

The Technical and Commercial Watershed. From an aesthetic point of view, letterpress and woodcut provided bold graphics, rapidly apprehended in the busy market place or shady tavern. In contrast, intaglio methods were able to produce graphics of greater refinement, better suited to wealthier markets in Amsterdam and London wanting to buy sheets for use in genteel music rooms. Unlike more cumbersome relief-blocks and moveable type, copper plates engraved with lyrics, imagery and notation had other, more practical commercial advantages: they were more easily stored and preserved in readiness for re-issue at a later date, and more faithfully reflected the nuances and fluidity of manuscript notation which was becoming increasingly complex. This development towards sophisticated intaglio notation, closely combined with comparable intaglio imagery and decoration is presaged in the remarkable work of engraver Johann Sadeler I (1550–1600), a hundred years before. *1.1*

By the 1690s, matters in the business improved still further when copper music engraving was superseded by speedier engraving and punch-work on more pliable pewter plates.

This revolution was welcomed by the growing numbers of printers and publishers. As competition amongst them increased, it became necessary for them to resort to the then novel means of advertising, albeit most often in the form of simple and cheap copy on their own title pages.

By about 1700, chapbooks (unbound, small format letterpress and woodcut collections of ballads) emerged at the lower end of the market. They must have rivalled the single-sided broadside with their similarity to the book and in their greater convenience and durability for both seller and buyer. They were without doubt, forerunners of the songsters which were letterpress lyric anthologies, most popular in the nineteenth and early twentieth centuries. At this time, a demand for simple, rapidly-printed music-sheets of opera and theatre songs arose. This might account for the decline in the use in ballads of the complex 'black-letter' type-face associated with Bible and legal printing, in favour of the less problematic, easier-to-cut and set 'white-letter' roman typeface.

Handel. In 1710, George Frederic Handel (1685–1759), came to London to find thriving professional and amateur communities of all classes delighting in orchestral and operatic concerts, *1.5* singing and ensemble playing. An influx of continental composers, performers, teachers and instrument makers winning noble and sometimes royal patronage made certain London was, by mid-century, one of the most important music publishing centres in Europe. After becoming 'Master of The Orchestra' of the Royal Academy of Music, Handel was in receipt of an unending line of commissions and popular adulation as a naturalised Englishman. In Handel's day, full scores, printed or otherwise, were still few and far between. Selections of songs from Handel's operas and sacred works were published, but in reduced forms sufficient to satisfy amateurs but deter performances by rival professional companies. Those who sought extra parts for instruments such as double basses, timpani and even trumpets were advised in title pages to '...*get in touch with M. Lallemand, the copyist of the Opera House.*[14]

Speedy publication of an admired work was essential for anyone seeking to reap full financial benefit. In a possible move to spoil the prospects of a proposed publication of an edition of his harpsichord suites on the Continent, and the probable circulation of unauthorised manuscript copies, Handel personally supervised a rapid printing of the work in London. The title page of this horizontal format work (published 1720), is devoid of imagery, content to display its quality, serious nature and good taste by way of engraved, calligraphic lettering which imitates the marks of a fine pen.[15]

Many composers wishing to publish work but lacking Handel's popularity and concomitant financial rewards often had to underwrite the publishers' costs of engraving, printing, binding and selling. This last expense might be as much as 25 per cent of the total cost so it was therefore common for works to be sold from the composer's own home.[16]

The new modes of retailing indigenous, printed luxury goods to a tutored, fashion-conscious market, particularly in London, coupled with a sage recognition of the need to supply the musically and socially ambitious with inspiring material as seen on the Continent, encouraged the production of a lot of high-quality material.[17] This led to a

competitive music publishing and printing environment producing in the middle of the eighteenth century, a second generation of entrepreneurs like Peter Welcker (d.1775), Robert Bremner (c.1713–89) and Domenico Corri (b. c.1746). The Haymarket premises owned by the *1.6.b,c* latter housed a free musical lounge and circulating library, which according to a woodcut and letterpress poster promoting it, consisted of a three-storey facade with its shop windows pasted-up with what were presumably currently available music-titles.[18]

Bickham Versus Cole. The profitable nature and creative aspects of song sheet-printing in eighteenth-century England are well illustrated by the case of the professional rivalry in London of George Bickham Junior (1706–71) and Benjamin Cole, a lesser-known engraver and publisher (active c.1730–60).[19]   *1.3 1.4*

The two volumes of The *Musical Entertainer* (1737–39), engraved by Bickham Junior comprised one hundred songs, (some by Handel), sold in parts, each carrying the name of a noted dedicatee, bass and treble clef notation, lyrics, figured bass and often a separate notational line for flute. The chief feature of these half-sheets are the delightful rococo headpieces in a decorative-figurative style known as *genre pittoresque*, typified by the work of the painter Jean-Antoine Watteau (1684–1721) which found rapid favour with the English who were knowingly appreciative of French taste and superior engraving skills.

In 1737 Bickham, having established a working relationship with the French designer Hubert François Gravelot (1699–1773), also began to issue 24 *octavo* sheets from a ballad farce called *Flora, or Hob in the Well,* engraved after Gravelot's specially commissioned drawings. Cole soon it giving rise to protracted public correspondence between them in the *Daily Advertiser.* The dispute escalated when Cole began to issue his *British Melody, or Cole's Musical Magazine* in deliberate formal imitation of Bickham's *Musical Entertainer.*

The affair highlights the familiarity at this date of insular engraver-publishers like Bickham with the designs and styling of French art, and of the apparent willingness of designers of the stature of Gravelot to participate (albeit on a limited scale) in the generation of English musical publications. In a bid to compete with the presence of the Frenchman, Cole may well have invented the   *15* 'incomparable Sig. Marini' cited as his Continental designer, in order to give some similar cachet of desirability to his sheets.

What is certainly revealed in the Bickham-Cole dispute is that a good deal of sophisticated critical comment was passed in respect of the technical and visual merits of the works in question which presumably would not be lost on readers of *The Daily Advertiser*. Indeed, Bickham writes of '...*Gentlemen and ladies of the most elegant taste and understanding in poetry, musick and engraving ...*' We find Bickham commenting upon imitations of his work which are '...*done in a very inaccurate Manner, and the designs prefix'd not in the least comparable to his, they being neither correct nor beautiful; ...*' Cole, countering in a comparable vein wrote of the '...*Impropriety of many of the Head-Pieces as not being well adapted to their respective Subjects...*' and of '...*the various errors and omissions in the musical Part of the Performance...*' What we see here is an example of double standards and professional rivalry with Bickham guiltlessly lifting and adapting French designs to suit his aims before criticising Cole for plagiarising his eclectic formula. Bickham took the opportunity of associating the songs with popular performers, fashionable venues and with subscribers or other persons of eminence. Such 'Star' associated promotional copy and deferential dedications witnessed here are to be seen again in later phases of music-selling.

Haydn. Joseph Haydn (1732–1809) arrived in England in 1791 but his work, most notably his *Set of Six Quartets,* Opus 1 as published in Amsterdam, had reached British shores 26 years earlier. What was probably an edition pirated from a manuscript copy was sold in London by Robert Bremner in 1765, who unreservedly advertised its availability widely in the press! The first English editions published with Haydn's permission were those of William Forster (1739–1808), music-printer and *'marchand'* who, like many other London music business traders, also sold musical instruments and was an instrument-maker to the King. An agreement of 1782 put the working relationship of Haydn and Forster on a firm footing. This did not, however, stop music-sellers and instrument makers to the Prince of Wales, Longman & Broderip (active c.1776–98), publishing rival editions with Haydn's connivance.

Longman & Broderip were a successful team running shops in Brighton, Margate and London.

They were astute enough to see the potential of a high public profile and to this end drove a van and horses with their names painted on the sides in large letters through the streets, thereby creating an impression of thriving trade in the minds of the public.[20]

On the title pages of eighteenth-century music publications we see the establishment of a marketing trait, already presaged in the sixteenth and seventeenth century use of broadside ballad-sheets as 'flyers' to promote song-books. This was the appearance in musical publications, not only of a publisher's own credentials and retailing address but of lists, complete with price and arrangement details of other new works of *'the following authors...'*. French publishers of the eighteenth century frequently went to the trouble of listing other works available on separate pages of particular titles, in effect creating efficient, low-cost advertising copy.

Detached, 'singleton' book frontispieces were often issued initially as 'advertising' prospectuses but became collectors' pieces almost immediately and had extended, independent lives circulating in bookshops.[21] It is not improbable that attractive music frontispieces might also have been sold separately in the same way, complementing the advertising role of the single sheet and prolonging the market exposure of composer, publisher and designer.

Rising demand for music both vocal and instrumental was further met by the many London periodicals like *The Gentleman's Magazine, The Universal Magazine, The London Magazine, The Lady's Magazine, The Royal Magazine* and *The European Magazine.* They all regularly carried music and songs, often featuring 'hits' from the theatre.

Designing, Printing and Selling Music in England, c.1790–c.1890

The Lithography Revolution. Increasing demands for clear, rapidly-executed printed music for all sectors of a lively European musical scene made it inevitable that sooner rather than later a new technique of replicating musical notation would be commercially developed. The technique chosen turned-out to be lithography, discovered in 1798 by Aloys Senefelder (1771–1834) and perfected and promoted by him in the following years in partnership with the music publishing firm of

André. Lithography is well suited to music replication as it is a more simple, more immediate alternative to engraving, involving a more natural, quickly-mastered autographic process on smooth limestone or transfer-paper surface. Although quick, easy and popular, this process never fully eclipsed established methods and had only a limited effect upon the publication of music in the more conservative 'serious' field, perhaps because it ultimately lacked the distinctness and intensity of intaglio or letterpress printing.

As had been the case in the 1690s when the introduction of engraving for notational printing had spilled-over into the decoration of title pages, the adoption of lithography by the trade in the early 1800s immediately drew the attentions of middle-rank publishers working in a mass-market field. Here, legibility and a visually attractive title page achieved equal status in the eyes of amateur performers of ambition and taste. The possibility of providing the 'perfect' means of decorating title pages with extravagant typography, untrammelled by grids, line and tone, in a manner akin to the freedoms of pencil or brush work had at last arrived.

George Cruikshank. Singled out here for spe-
1.10.a,b cial attention is George Cruikshank (1792–1878), several of whose prints and preparatory drawings for musical publications are now preserved in the V & A Museum. A popular and prolific illustrator, he almost totally eschewed the subtleties of lithography and the forcefulness of woodcuts in favour of wood-engraving and etching. He generated a tremendous number of images for all manner of works on paper ranging from caricatures and lottery tickets, through to illustrations for Dickens' novels, each one striking the necessary visual chord, not least in those serving the music business. The periodic issue of musical part-works or anthologies fronted by engraved or etched plates by Cruikshank, and others of well-loved contemporary comic, romantic, national song toasts and sentiments, became increasingly popular as up-
1.11.a,b market counterparts of the chapbook. Publications illustrated by Cruikshank include: '*Smeeton's Selection of the most approved Songs for 1809 ... As Sung at Vauxhall, Haymarket, Sadler's Wells Circus, Astley's etc...written by Mr. Dibdin and Sung by Mr. Grimaldi ...*' and '*Bailey's New Song Book For the Present Year, containing the most Choice, Favourite, Popular and Celebrated Songs now singing with Great applause at the*

Theatres Royal, and minor places of amusement, etc., etc.,' (1816).

Part-works answered demands from less wealthy amateurs for a standardised product easily secured at regular intervals. For such amateurs, possession of the latest pieces was a social necessity made doubly attractive by their relative cheapness and the comparative ease with which they could subsequently be bound together.

Cruikshank's graphics were more than visual diversions. Their characterful linearity imbued the books and sheets with 'added-value' and thus added desirability in an age when writers and painters in Britain were also engaged in the production of highly descriptive texts and canvases.

Catnach and Pitts the Flying Stationers.[22] Like Cruikshank, most broadside-printers chose not to experiment with the new technique of lithography but for different reasons. They relied on a regular turnover of hundreds of cheap, letterpress-broadsides sold to poor, conservatively-minded customers. The adoption of lithography by these *1.9* printers would have radically changed the product and would have led to price-rises to cover the costs of new plant. Even the most successful flying stationers, James Catnach (1792–1841) and John Pitts (1765–1844), remained loyal to traditional letterpress and relief-block methods for their predominantly urban, musically-illiterate market. It seems that only the superficial form of the broadside was important, any image, however irrelevant might serve as a headpiece. These pictures were nevertheless there, as before to impart an aesthetic dimension to the sheets which was of great significance for the many consumers wanting not just words but pictures suitable for decorating the walls of their homes.

Who determined the appearance of these relief-print broadsides? Lyricists living a precarious hand-to-mouth existence would have no opportunity or wish to be associated too closely with an individual printer-publisher. Similar considerations would operate for tunesmiths who, in any case, would not be able to dictate the use of their unscored melodies. Printers and publishers made the greatest contribution to the appearance of the ballads, selecting the type, headpieces, paper and inks. In reality there were many instances of irrelevant images atop lyrics, many spelling mistakes and substitute and inverted type characters resulting from hasty work, poor organisation and a cavalier attitude to standards.

Pitts, Catnach and their immediate successors dominated this end of the music publishing business in London throughout the nineteenth century. They worked out of The Seven Dials, an area noted in the first half of the century for the prominent activities of its street-literature authors, printers and ballad-mongers. The latter complemented the points of sale booths, shops and cleft sticks of Cheapside, Bow Church Yard and West Smithfield. Ballads were actually sold by numerous 'pinners-up', some claiming to sell as many as one hundred and fifty on a fine day from their palings, lines or gaudily painted boards and poles. Ballads were frequently sold 'by the yard', lines of sheets being pasted together so they might billow in the breeze. Others not sold at Catnach's counter or on the immediate streets of The Seven Dials would be taken-up by retailers owning sweetshops, tobacco shops, toy shops and the like.[23] Pitts, having established himself in the Seven Dials by 1802, discovered, on the arrival of Catnach in c.1814 (who had brought superior blocks and type from his parents' established printing firm in the North of England), the need to re-appraise the quality of his product. He set aside his rough, blue and green tinted papers, mixture of lamp-black and oil for higher quality sheets and proper printer's ink.

The rivalry between these two men was intense, but unlike that between Bickham and Cole, was resolved in the market place in a fiercely competitive mood of commercial pride and industry. In fact Catnach was able to stay ahead of Pitts, dominating the business until his retirement in 1838. Catnach, who issued some three thousand titles during his career (his 1832 catalogue lists some seven hundred titles and 15 song-books), is said to have sent employees in to rural areas to track-down and record new material suitable for publication. Many baladeers lived in and around The Seven Dials district and made regular contributions to the trade with Catnach employing a fiddler to test the efficacy of new works which, if liked would initially be paired-up on sheets with 'standards' which were guaranteed to sell.

Catnach operated with a maximum of four presses, each chase taking two forms at a time, a set-up capable of printing some one thousand titles an hour. Although he probably used stereotypes for some of his headpieces, he must also have relied on wood-engravers to generate the necessary imagery. Some impressions from Catnach's presses carry the name of the wood-engraver Thomas Bewick (1753–1828). He also produced his own crude blocks carved in the backs of old pewter music-plates, nailed onto blocks of wood then set in the press.

The relatively unsophisticated 'folk art' of the broadsides of Catnach and Pitts could not begin to capture the beauty or presence of a 'star' performer but neither could Cruikshank's frenetic, caricature-inspired images produced by wood-engraving or etching. Engraving (on steel from the 1820s) could not offer a solution being too slow and formal while any etched, aquatint images would be too slight and delicate in appearance.[24]

Colour lithography. The advent of colour lithography in the 1840s led many music publishers to dedicate the whole of the song-sheet cover to a richly-coloured lithography image illustrating either the performer, a domestic or outdoor scene (if such were the song's subject), or a depiction of music-making and dances. The reliance on sentiment, patriotism, comedy and fashionable, domestic pursuits had already been witnessed in the eighteenth-century half-sheets of Bickham and Cole. They were now, however, less demure and more sweet and colourful, so that they might compete effectively with the growing number magazines, books and newspapers on offer.

1.17.a,b

A keen rivalry was displayed by the music publishers in issuing attractive frontispieces, it being a maxim with some of them that "a good picture sells a piece."

So wrote Imeson in the first book to survey illustrated song-sheets of this period which he wrote in 1912, based on contact made with some those who had been involved in their production.[25]

Colour lithography exerted the talents of a large number of draughtsmen in the nineteenth century, with perhaps Alfred Concanen (1835–86) becoming the most well-known in Britain. Concanen's early works were produced in conjunction with Thomas Wales Lee (1833–1910), a fellow lithographer responsible for the typographical and decorative forms on the sheets. Working with Concanen and Lee was Walter Roberts Mallyon (b.1840) whose talents also stretched to the designing of theatrical posters. Experiments with photolithography throughout most of the nineteenth century, culminating with the half-tone screen in the 1880s, had no discernible impact on the face of song-sheets until the beginning of the twentieth century, when it was coupled with the economic advantages of rotary offset printing.

Among those specialising in song-sheet illustration was John Brandard (1812–63), who produced fine-quality colour lithography images on high grade paper for the show business entrepreneur Louis Jullien (1812–60). Employing two assistants to prepare the stones and furnish him with smooth surfaces, they worked too on minor detailing and shading. Being anxious to retain his services, the publishers M. & N. Hanhart (who were Brandard's sole employers for a number of years), granted him considerable freedom, often sanctioning the use of six or more stones to create one rich and colourful design.

Several musicians and composers took part in the generation of colour lithography song-sheet imagery. Examples are Charles Lyall (1833–1911) who was a noted operatic singer adept as a draftsman in intaglio and planographic techniques as was William Michael Watson (1840-89), composer and songwriter.

Stars, Pirates and Libraries in the Nineteenth Century.

> In England, publishers pay vocalists to popularize a song, either by a specified fee per night or a royalty on copies sold, for a specified term or perhaps for the duration of the copyright. Vocalists stamp their name on each copy in order to check the numbers sold, the much criticized "royalty system".
> *Musical Opinion & Music Trade Review,*
> March, 1889, p. 296. [26]

Intensified urbanisation and industrialisation brought about a rise in new recreational habits. In towns and cities of the 1840s, the music halls emerged as a key venues for variety shows centred around serious and comic singers, who would often receive royalties, have their ballad concerts subsidised or be in receipt of other inducements if they promoted a particular song. At the same time there was an increase in piano manufacture and in the number of piano and singing lessons, the latter using the simple 'tonic sol-fa' system of notation (still in use in the 1950s). The introduction of the piano into thousands of homes by the end of the century combined with the popularity of singing at home inevitably increased demand for decorative, printed editions of popular pieces. [27]

Amateur and professional choral groups sprang-up as did brass band societies and new orchestral concert series like those of the Hallé. At the same time, large prestigious city festivals took place alongside the more informal attractions of the music hall creating a fertile mix of musical fare which appealed to all classes. Improved means of travel and rising educational standards accelerated the homogenisation of tastes in urban life which demanded standardised, good-quality music and regular spectacles. To match changing opportunities, the business strategies of music publishers became increasingly premeditated. Novello's (founded 1811), saw that people would be less inclined to hand-copy printed scores if they could buy cheap editions. They therefore began to issue inexpensive music in the 1840s, a move which immediately goaded rivals into action. In 1858, Chappell's (founded 1811) initiated and financed the building of St. James' Hall, Piccadilly and later supported The D'Oyly Carte Theatre's productions of operettas by W. S. Gilbert (1842–1900) and A. S. Sullivan (1836–1911), whose music they published. The demand for cheap music could not be fully met by legitimate methods so the age-old problem of piracy surfaced again but on a larger scale.

The Holy City was published legitimately at the start of the twentieth century by Boosey & Co. who successfully brought a case against J. Poole & Son for printing, without permission, five thousand copies of the work. It was conceded that some forty to fifty thousand copies of the popular composition had been issued by them and others had been sold at a variety of prices. The inferior nature of the pirate copies was revealed in the May 1903 edition of the *Musical Opinion & Music Trade Review*:

> The illicit copy of, say, *The Holy City* betrays a common and vulgar style of printing...When placed on a pianoforte in any respectable drawing room or music room it would be shabbily out of place...They are produced in facsimile by a photographic process...principally in Liverpool...then sold in the provinces chiefly house to house. [28]

Retailers opened musical libraries to generate income and presumably generate sales. One such library was that of Ewer & Co., of Regent Street, *'Music Sellers to the Queen...'* (starting-out as importers of music in c.1824), who begged *'to recommend their Universal Circulating Musical Library'* to teachers and amateurs in a press advertisement of c.1865. [29] Boasting the possession of

51,801 different works, the library claimed to be modelled on the best continental institutions, introducing to *'subscribers the whole range of Musical Publications, both classical and ephemeral'*. Music retailer J. Bath of Great Marlborough Street London, rubber-stamped the blank inner-page of a song-sheet of c.1879, *The Garnet Wolsey* (V&A Museum, E. 754–1947), with short and simple promotional copy for other titles. One of these stamps publicising *'He was a Careful Man'* includes the following recommendation from *The Times*: *'It is an excellent song and deserves its popularity.'* In addition to using high-profile promotional ruses appearing on printed music matter itself, many publishers and retailers relied on advertisements in the regular press and in trade publications, and would also rely on brief credit-lines in the many songsters of the period.

Number 357 of *The Monthly Musical Budget* of September 1905, published by F. Pitman Hart & Co. Ltd., is an example of a music periodical encompassing many of the sales tactics of the period as well as pitches favoured in earlier centuries. This one penny publication sought to have something for everyone, containing: *'Songs sentimental and humorous, piano, dance and harmonium music.'* Other Pitman Hart publications including tutor-books, are advertised in its pages, together with a promotional display for back-copies containing compositions by the popular Charles Gounod. Also advertised in this somewhat lack-lustre periodical is an elaborate work entitled *Domestic Ditties* replete with thirty colour illustrations. Page ten of this *Monthly Musical Budget* carries a note on the submission of manuscripts which throws some light upon publication practices at this date: *'Composers and writers...are requested to state what payment, if any, is required for the Mss...or whether the same are offered for gratuitous insertion.'* Other pages carry advertisements for performers and musical accessories as well as twelve 'sample' bars from a newly-published mazurka. Evidence that competition, both legal and piratical was fierce is suggested in copy which states that for sale were *'Not pirated but genuine editions of new numbers...reduced from 4/- to sixpence each...'*

In McGlennon's *Record Songbook* no.143, a descendant of the songster issued in about 1942, we see the usual writer and publisher credits to promote sales and careers, but in addition the following warning appears: *'Notice to Printers,*

Dance promoters, &c. The Songs in this Publication are copyright and must not be reprinted without the consent in writing of the copyright owners.' It is followed by the names of six people successfully prosecuted for copyright infringement together with the fines or prison sentences they received. This same edition lists points of sale which include the establishments of the copyright holders, wholesalers and *'local musical stockists'*.

Designing, Printing and Selling Music in North America.[30]

In the Beginning. The so-called *Bay Psalm Book* issued in New England in 1640, was the first musical publication of the New World. The edition, devoid of notation had a print-run of some 1,700 copies and was re-issued 11 years later. America's first printed musical notes appeared in the 1698 *New Edition of Psalms, Hymns and Spirituals* modelled on John Playford's *Introduction to the Skill of Music.* (1654). This psalm book, together with imported psalm and secular books was available to the buying public of Boston at outlets like Michael Perry's bookstore. The over-all commercial picture before 1781 was generally one of little development. Paper and press importation difficulties resulting from conflict with Britain, combined with the vital need to settle the land, severely limited the production, appreciation and purchase of printed music. However parts of the East Coast colonies' secular music business did flourish. An example is that of exiled Englishman, Thomas Fleet (d.1758), based in Boston, who used an English press and type-faces to issue English and American broadside-ballads illustrated with some of his own headpieces.

The East Coast Publishing Bonanza, c.1781–c.1920. Cultural consumption in eighteenth-century America had been almost exclusively Euro-centric. Printed music was ordered from the few specialist music shops set up by the London publishers, and shipped across the Atlantic to be performed on imported European instruments. The War of Independence (1775–81), stimulated the nascent American music business into creating a healthy publishing trade to feed a growing national market. This, followed by the emergence of a lively dance and musical theatre tradition centred on indigenous and European music, did much to encourage the appearance of music in print. Many printers, publishers and retailers were keen to exploit the advantages of newly-adopted musical type, lax copyright laws and improving transport and mail networks.

From the 1820s, lithography gained a hold on the mass-market sector of the business, boosted by an interest in minstrel songs, parlour songs and early vaudeville. Introduction of colour lithography by Bostonians William Sharp and John H. Bufford in the 1840s, with some of the finest sheets issued in wrappers and titled-cases, gave the American music business a further tonic, laying the foundations for the large scale, conventionally organised music houses operating at extremely competitive levels out of Boston, Philadelphia and New York.

The music retailer Oliver Ditson of Boston (1811–88), sold his material using established links with consumers made through two thousand retail outlets, music-paper advertisements, booklets and thematic lists, sent by post all-over North America.

In spite of the rapaciousness of the large houses, there was still space enough for local music stores to offer the unknown composer basic printing and retailing facilities. Emerging in the 1880s, Tin Pan Alley, New York's song factory employed a host of professional song writers, which relied heavily on repetition and aggressive sales techniques of trained travelling salesmen to move its products.

As in Britain, the key to the selling of American music has always been the repetition over a short period of promising material in the presence of potential consumers. This was achieved through live performances by a 'star', supported initially by the distribution of low-grade, un-adorned 'artists copies' and instrumental dance arrangements of the tunes, in advance of any full-scale release. In the 1890s, 'nickel-odeon' disc musical-boxes, and later, phonographs and player pianos, shared the task of bringing 'the hook' of a tune to the customer's ears. In the March 21st. 1903 issue of the American show business paper *Billboard*, the Boswell Optical Co. of Chicago announced that it was selling *Steropticon* projectors and *'illustrated song slides...Beautifully coloured 25c each'*. These were projected at vaudeville theatres like the four hundred seat Novelty Theatre in Minneapolis featured in *Billboard*, March 20th 1909, a phenomenon which no doubt further contributed to the subsequent sheet sales of featured Tin Pan Alley tunes.

All of the American song-sheets from c.1900 to the 1920s are bold, optimistic illustrations of comic lyrics, performers, well-healed society people, dancers and romancers. Their colour range tends to be limited, lending emphasis to the stylised, synthetic and theatrical, self-contained aspect of the work of busy designers like Natwick, E.H. Pfeiffer and Barbelle whose names litter sheets at this date.[31] As ever, songs had to address popular preoccupations, arouse the emotions and be be arranged in the predominant musical style of the day. The song-sheet covers inevitably had a central role in communicating such content and we therefore see illustrations of aeroplanes, soldiers off to war and society couples romantically entwined, together with the more realistic depictions of 'stars' like Sophie Tucker (1884–1966) and Al Jolson (1886–1950).

Perhaps a more demanding challenge for designers was the arrival of ragtime. Rags were initially just rhythmical, instrumental pieces of negro origin well-suited to the piano. Many were devoid of lyrics and it fell to the composers, and probably publishers and designers employed in the Tin Pan Alley commercialisation of the rag (and indeed other 'crazes') to devise an imaginative title which could be effectively rendered in graphic terms. An example of this is Starmmer's illustration of a collapsing piano for Karl Kaffe's *Going to Pieces Rag* published in 1915. Rags had, from the beginning, interested 'serious' composers and designers. In 1919, Picasso (1881–1973) produced a cover for the piano arrangement of *Ragtime* by Igor Stravinsky (1882–1971).[32]

Sheet sales in America were paramount for publisher's profits until the 1920 paper shortage and printer's strike. As early as 1919 we see song-sheet copy informing consumers that numbers were also available as a phonograph record and player-piano music-rolls – just *'...ask your dealer'*.

Film-makers buoyant with the success of the 'talkies' in the late 1920s, proceeded to buy-up or buy-into established music-publishing enterprises, seeing the need to gain a stronger foothold in the entertainment business. The Depression in the 1930s marked the end of the dominance of the song-sheet as a primary material form for the selling of the immaterial to a musically-active consumer. Instead, radio and to a lesser extent cinema, live dance bands and later records, took over as entertainment and commodity, between them setting the musical agenda for decades to come.

1.14.a,b, *18.b*

The transitional nature of the music business in the 1930s is exemplified by the radio 'Hit Parade' chart wherein the positions of 'the hits' were determined by a combination of radio airplay, record sales, juke-box plays and song-sheet sales. Musical taste of the passive majority in post-war America and Europe was being catered for largely by the radio, juke-box, record player, dances and to some extent the local live music scene. Raw musical talent now went straight to the record company, only later having a need to work with publishers.[33] Those with a desire to perform might begin by imitating established 'stars' and playing cover-versions of popular songs but would soon want to be composing and performing their own material. Harmonically and melodically advanced material which, before World War II had been adapted naturally for the parlour-piano or dance-band, was patently not conducive to the commercially promising, youth-oriented rock and roll line-up of drums and guitars.

Jazz of the swing era, which had been composed and arranged for big dance bands and vocalists was being eclipsed in avant garde quarters by the work of bebop and later free-jazz musicians whose advanced musical idioms could not be faithfully translated into 'dots' on a page. Those active in this sphere sought-out tutor-books, scale-books, 'fake-books' and recordings by the likes of Stravinsky from which they made their own study-transcripts.

So many song-sheets produced after the war have a distinctly fatigued, monochromatic, appearance. Over-reliant on photography, and reflecting the economic realities of the music-publishing business, sheet-music became simply the physical embodiment of copyright declarations.

The revival of the artistic quality of printed popular music began in the 1950s and '60s when musically-innovative and popular artists like Elvis Presley (1935–77), Frank Sinatra (b.1915), Bob Dylan (b.1941), Stevie Wonder (b.1950), and The Beatles (1962–70), became money-spinners in all quarters of the music business, justifying the publication of 'big-production' song-folios. These were anthologies which, in terms of their cover imagery sensibly echoed record sleeve designs and which were peppered with interviews and exclusive photographs in bids to rival the ubiquitous 'fake-book'.[34] This formula has continued to the present day, with many song-books being

1.19.a,b

glossy picture-books aimed at the 'pop' magazine market rather than musical transcriptions for amateur or semi-professional use.

Tutor-books, budget and 'period' anthologies still abound, riding on the wave of the continued popularity of the guitar and major advances in home-keyboard technology. They contain gutted arrangements of songs, spiral-bound and fronted by brightly-illustrated covers which stress the ease by which the 'sophisticated' and authentic works within can be mastered. The economic recession of the late 1970s saw music houses fall back onto the sale of educational material and arrangements of pop and rock songs for general consumption. Unlike their classical music counterparts which can be placed on shelves or in drawers for long-term sale, these song-books are displayed like records in wooden racking or on rotating metal racks, clearly visible to the browsing customer in specialist retail or departmental stores. They can also be sold successfully by mail-order. In the 1970s and '80s, the publishing of single sheets by large American houses like Screen Gems, Columbia Publications, Warner Brothers Music and The Big Three (United Artists) depended less on the reputation of a performer than on a 45 rpm record release reaching the top one hundred singles chart.

Designing, Printing and Selling 'Serious' Music after 1945.

The selling of 'serious' art music began with entrepreneurs like Playford, Walsh, Forster, Breitkopf, Schott *et al* and became firmly established in the nineteenth century with formidable publications coming-out of houses like Ricordi in Italy and G. Schirmer in America.

Early this century, when the visual arts and music moved closer together, designs for some 'serious' compositions were given a contemporary look when for example the composer Paul Hindemith (1895–1964) placed his own busy, expressionistic design on the cover of his *Piano Suite* Opus 26. Georges Braque (1882–1963), designed a beautifully restrained lithographic frontispiece for *Léger Commme un Oeuf* composed by Erik Satie (1866–1925), whilst Francis Picabia (1879–1935) designed the frontispiece for Satie's *Relâche.*

1.18.a

Since World War II, publication of music for the professional performer and scholar has tended to rely on the photolithographic re-issue of facsimile or near-facsimile editions of the original publications or of re-issues of exhaustively researched, pre-war editions of international repute. The precedents for such historical editions go back to series like Arnold's *Handel Edition* (1787–97), The Musical Antiquarian Society's two-volume *Popular Music of the Olden Time* (1855–9) and the Peters Edition series begun in 1867.

Overt fidelity to form in the facsimile field (be it the reproduction of original covers or scores), lays indirect stress on authenticity, continuity and authority; all of them characteristics vaunted by publishers and desired by consumers. Meanwhile the use of elegant but standard passe-partout frames, titles and formats for a series establishes an all-important uniformity that suggests that the work is a single, 'incomplete' component of a larger commodity. Faber's editions of music by Benjamin Britten (1913–76) after World War I were highly-regarded for their laboriously produced but crystal-clear scores created by teams using the Halstan process of stencils, photographic reduction and offset printing.

Some publishers tend to repeat the established record sleeve formula of placing a portrait of the composer on the cover, while at the same time, preserving a degree of typographic restraint to reflect the 'clean-cut' score within. Others adopt ruses from the sheet-music field of an earlier century, reproducing this time, not a performer's signature, but that of the composer, as with the 1979 Novello edition of early part-songs by Sir Edward Elgar (1857–1934). Some designs use well-know imagery from earlier centuries, enlivening them with bright, modern colouring. An example here is the case of the Dover Edition of the *Fitzwilliam Virginal Book* of c.1979, an unabridged reproduction of the Breitkopf & Härtel edition of 1899. It reproduces the William Hole (active 1612–18) cover of the *Parthenia* virginal book of 1612–13, the first English music publication to be graced with an engraved image.

In keeping with the 1950s trend of employing noted designers to work on covers for living composers, we see Neville Brody (b.1957) producing a cover for *New Year,* an opera by Sir Michael Tippett (b.1905) published in 1989 by Schott & Co.

1.21.b

It is interesting to observe that in the twentieth century, progressive modes of 'serious' composition and performance have necessitated the development of new notational symbols and patterns of layout. These have frequently attempted to ally their informational content with a contributory visual aesthetic. A prime example of this is seen in some scores by John Cage (b.1912), for example: *Fontana Mix* (1958) and *Sixty-two Mesostics Re Merce Cunningham* (1971). *Artikulation,* (1958) by György Ligeti (b.1923) has its own 'listening score' wherein coloured shapes and symbols attempt to present the listener with a progressive, visual representation of the sound envelopes, note clusters and timbres of the piece.

1.15.a,b

Such works are however the exception. It is acknowledged by some publishers that the appearance of conventional, computer-set editions is the result of a need to satisfy copyright regulations rather than a wish to encourage purchase, study and performance. Could it be that music-publishing is no-longer an area for graphic innovation and large-scale profit? Is it now yet another 'service industry' which, in its chosen market is more reactive than creative?

Notes:

1   See Dart,T. (1967) pp. 11–12; King, A. H. (1979) p. 7 and Attali, J. (1985) p.37.

2   See Searle, A. (1987) and Arts Council of Great Britain (1986) for accounts of the history and continued importance of manuscript music.

3   For a thorough survey of the nature and extent of improvised music-making in the West see Bailey, D. (1980).

4   It is known that in 1532, the French composer Carpentras (c.1470–1536), had a type-face of his invention cut for the printing of two collections of his sacred works. In the nineteenth century, Carl Maria von Weber (1786–1826), lithographed his *Piano Variations,* Opus 2 with Richard Wagner (1813–83) doing likewise for the full score of *Tannhäuser.* See King, A. H. (1979) p. 28.

5   In the publishing contract for Beethoven's *Three Trios for Piano,* Opus 1, the composer stated that the edition should be attractive and have a decorative title: '*rein und schön auch mit einem zierlichen titelblatte versehen.*' Fraenkel, G. S. (1968) plate 197.

6   MS. e̜ Mus. 198, Bodleian Library Oxford.

7   The *Constance Gradual* is now in the British Library. *A New Song for the City of Rothenberg* c.1520 by Erhard Schoen (c.1491–1542), is an example of a woodcut-broadside. It is reproduced in Bartsch (1984) no. 240.

8 This monopoly is reproduced in Wulstan, D. (1985) p. 25. For the statistics on ballad registration see Neuberg, V. E. (1977) pp. 37–8.

9 There was in fact much activity in the publication of psalm setting, yet publishers had much recourse to design motifs, (especially printers fleurons and the all-pervasive passe-partout frame) taken from blocks of earlier decades. Was this an economic move or a deliberate attempt to evoke sentiments of simplicity?

10 On a Playford advertisement see Coral, L. (1967).

11 Playford, *Select Ayres And Dialogues* (1659), cited Spink, I. (1986) pp. 131–3.

12 Cited Spink, I. (1986) p. 217.

13 See prints by the likes of Andries Both (c.1618–52), Cornelis Dusart (1660–1704) and Nicholas Van Haften (c.1663–1715). For the pasting-up of broadside ballads in the eighteenth century see Martin, M. (1987) pp. 343–61.

14 Dart, T. (1975) p. 67.

15 Horizontal formats presented wider pages to those dealing with notation, who could thereby set-down long musical phrases. Broken phrasing is undesirable from the point of view of a performer.

16 Fisk, R. (1973) p. 295.

17 Music-books engraved in eighteenth-century France set standards for the rest of Europe too. Prestigious publications would often be the result of collaborations between a number of designers, calligraphers and engravers. The greatest achievement in this area is said to be La Borde's *Choix de Chansons* published in Paris (1773), a technically perfect work completed without punches which carries a number of full-page illustrative engravings to accompany the songs. See Poole, H. E. and Krummel, D.W. (1980) p. 253.

18 Illustrated Weill, A. (1985) p. 15.

19 See Snodin, M. (1983) pp. 355–9 and Valpy, N. (1989) pp. 54–9.

20 Fiske, R. (1973) p. 300.

21 See Van Der Waals, J. (1984).

22 I have relied consistently on two works for the factual data in this section: Hindley, C. H. (1970) and Shepard, L. (1969). This second title furnishes useful information on the precursors of Pitt and Catnach.

23 For the sale of songs on the streets of nineteenth century France see Attali, J. (1985) pp. 73–4.

24 Aquatinted covers were, in one sense the transitional stage between the engraved headpieces of the eighteenth century and the hand-coloured or colour lithography song-sheets of the nineteenth century. See Haill, C. (1981) p. 3.

25 Imeson, W. E. (1912) p. 7.

26 Cited Coover, J. (1985) p. 40.

27 For thorough accounts of the British musical scene in the nineteenth century, see the following from which many of the factual details given here are taken: Pearsall, R. (1973) and Russell, D. (1987). For further discussion of music halls see chapter 2.

28 Cited in Coover, J. (1985) pp. 87 & 103–4. Coover adds: *'there are eighteen printed editions of The Holy City, some mere blotches. Pirates it is claimed, can print cheaply 500,000 copies, and stand to lose little even if some are confiscated.'*

29 V&A Museum, E. 1328–1990.

30 Much of the historical background and factual content of this section is drawn from the following: Sanjek, R. (1984) and (1988); Poole, H. E. and Krummel, D. J. (1980) pp. 232–74 and Krummel, D. W. (1986) pp. 650–4.

31 See Wilk, M. (1973).

32 The former illustrated Wilk, M. (1973) p.62, the latter Fraenkel, G. S. (1968) p. xxxi.

33 The importance of disc sales is well illustrated with the following figures: In 1958, $511m worth of records were sold in comparison to $30m worth of sheet music. Cited Sanjek, R. (1980) p.47.

34 Examples of 'photo' song-books aimed at the amateur market are *The Rolling Stones Song Book* with *'exclusive new photos and six hit songs.'* (c.1965); *A Score of Buddy Holly*, with seven full-page pin-ups and a portrait drawn by James Wishart (1963) and *The Buddy Holly Souvenir Album* with biography and pin-ups. (1961 and reprinted late '60s). Copies of all three are in the V&A's Theatre Museum, Rock and Pop Archive. Alongside song-books with musical notation are 'fine-art' collections of words on their own such as *More Dark than Shark* (1986), a book of Russell Mills paintings that illustrate lyrics by Brian Eno and *Poguetry*, The Lyrics of Shane MacGowan (of the Pogues), illustrated by John Hewitt and Steve Pyke (1989). Both published by Faber & Faber.

PLATE 1.1 : So-called picture-motet. *The Virgin and Child with Saint Anne.* Ex: Johann Sadeler I
(1550–1600), after a painting by Marten de Vos (1531/2–1603). Engraving. Published in Antwerp
in 1584, re-issued in Rome in 1586 and again in Antwerp in 1587. Cut to: 25.2 x 19.7. E. 5413–1919.
Active across Europe, Sadeler was responsible for several devotional sheets of exceptional quality
like this which is one of the earliest dated examples of engraved music. The wholly successful
juncture of engraved notation and finely engraved imagery presages work in later centuries.

Plate 1.2.a : Frontispiece. (probably a nineteenth-century copy). *The Nightingale Sheretine and Mariana...[etc.].* Songs and Sonnets by Patrick Hannay, Gent. Ex: Crispin van de Passe. Engraving. Printed for Nathaniel Butter (sic) for the poet Hannay (d.1629?). 1622. Possibly The Hunterian Club facsimile published in 1875. 15.6 x 9.4. E. 1921–1886.

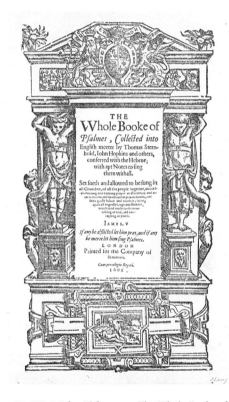

PLATE 1.2.b: Title page. *The Whole Booke of Psalmes.* Des: anon. Woodcut. Printed for the Company of Stationers, London. 1606. 27.0 x 17.0. 16409. The architectural frame was a common compositional device seen on title pages across Europe in the late-sixteenth and early-seventeenth century.

A part of the copy states that the psalms were *'conferred with the Hebrue, with apt notes to sing them together...after morning prayer...and moreover in private houses, for their Godly solace and comfort, laying apart all unGodly songs and balades, which lend onely to the nourishing of vice, and corrupting of youth.'*

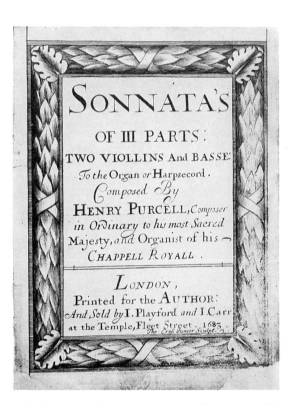

PLATE 1.2.c : Title page. *Henry Purcell's Sonnata's of III Parts.* Ex: Thomas Cross Junior (active c.1660–65). Engraving. Pub: Purcell, sold by John Playford (active 1623–86), and John Carr. London 1683. Plate-mark: c.22.6 x 16.8. British Museum.

PLATE 1.3 : Two So-called half-sheets. From *The Musical Entertainer*, Vol. I. *The Inamour'd Swain* and *Love's Bacchanal*. Des. & ex: George Bickham Junior (1706?–1771). Etching and engraving. Pub. & pr: Bickham. 1738. Plate-marks: 32.4 x 19.8 and 32.4 x 22.0. E. 1191, 1192–1983. Representative plates from the publication reflecting French taste in rococo England. The headpiece of the second plate shows, in reverse, a setting copied from Jean Mondon's *Sixième Livre De Formes Rocailles … [etc.]* 1736. Note the dedications, figured bass and lines for flute.

PLATE 1.4 : Six so-called half-sheets. Des. & ex: Benjamin Cole (active c.1730–60). Etching and engraving. Pub. & pr: Cole. Average size of sheets: 20.3 x 12.0. E. 105, 102, 108, 109, 111, 113–1972. Compare to plate 1.3. Note the ever-present themes of pastoral love, the fashionable interior and patriotism.

The COMPARISON set to Music, the WORDS by a Young LADY.

Love & Freedom.

Rouse Brittons.

Sung by Mr. Beard.

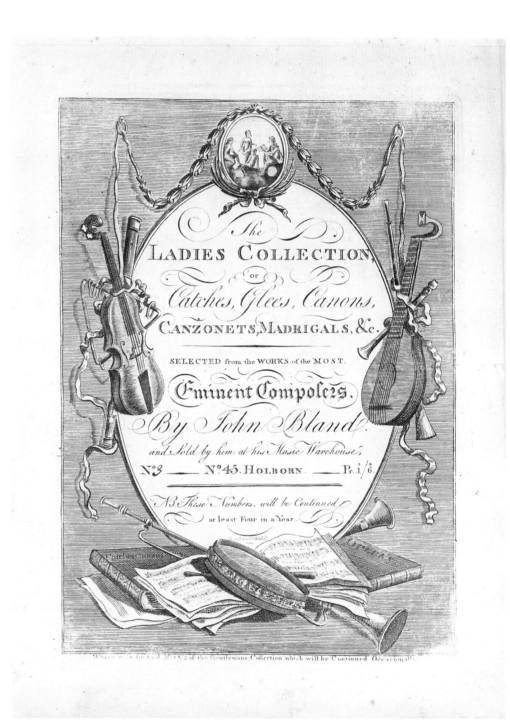

PLATE 1.5 : Title page. *The Ladies Collection of Catches, Glees,... [etc.].*
Ex: Boyce (Possibly Sammuel Boyce, d.1775). Etching and engraving. Mid-eighteenth
century. Plate-mark: 28.0 x 20.3. E. 2681–1921. A part-work designed to appeal to
society women singing in groups and rivalling men's singing societies popular at this
date. Note the 'English guitar' at the right of the frame which is a form of cittern,
an easy-to-master-instrument often associated with women amateurs.

PLATE 1.6.a : Trade-card. *John Johnston*
Music Engraver & Instrument Maker.
(active in 1760s and 1770s). Ex: W. Sherwin.
Etching and engraving. 7.6 x 10.8. 12875.2.
Johnston's business was eventually bought-
up by publishing giants Longman & Broderip.

1.6.b : Trade-card. *Peter Welcker.* (d.1775) Des: anon.
Etching and engraving. Plate-mark: 14.3 x 8.4. 12860.2. The copy
informs customers of the availability on *'reasonable terms'*
of musical instruments, new music, and the service of music
copying and book binding. In 1764, Welcker introduced the
single-volume score, removing the need for separate part-
books, an innovation rapidly and widely imitated. Welcker's
catalogue was bought-up by Robert Bremner in 1779.

1.6.c : Billhead. *Robert Bremner.* (c.1713–1789). Des:
anon. Engraving. 1768. 11.2 x 22.3. E. 232–1943. Note that
this receipt is headed by a sign-board which would have
been superceded in 1762 by the numbering of London
premises. Bremner died in 1789 having established a
successful business fronted by shops in the Strand,
London and in Brighton.

Trade-cards were printed on fine-quality paper, distributed
with deliveries and given-away or
sold at trade counters. These
examples impart service
information and through their
styling, inform customers of the
engraver and retailer's wishes to
be viewed as fashion-conscious,
educated craftsmen. These
examples are for the period,
stylistically restrained, serving as
plainer adjuncts to the florid,
promotional aspects of many
contemporary music-titles.

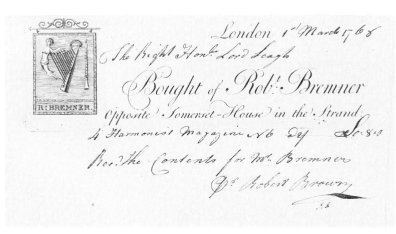

The Roaſt Beef of Old England. A CANTATA. By YOUNG D'URFEY.

RECITATIVE.

'TWAS at the Gates of *Calais*, HOGARTH tells,
Where ſad Deſpair and Famine always dwells,
A meagre Frenchman, *Madam Grandſire*'s Cook,
As Home he ſteer'd his Carcaſe, that way took,
Bending beneath the Weight of fam'd *Sir-Loin*,
On whom he often wiſh'd in vain to dine;
Good Father *Dominick* by chance came by,
With ruſty Gills, round Paunch, and greedy Eye,
Who, when he firſt beheld the greaſy Load,
His Benediction on it he beſtow'd;
And, while the ſolid Fat his Finger preſs'd,
He lick'd his Chaps, and thus the Knight addreſs'd:

AIR.

A lovely Laſs to a Friar came, &c.

O rare *Roaſt Beef!* lov'd by all Mankind,
If I was doom'd to have thee,
When dreſs'd and garniſh'd to my Mind,
And ſwimming in thy Gravy,
Not all thy Country's Force combin'd
Should from my Fury ſave thee.
Renown'd *Sir-Loin*, oft times decreed
The Theme of Engliſh Ballad,
E'n Kings on thee have deign'd to feed,
Unknown to Frenchman's palate;
Then how much more thy Taſte exceeds
Soup-meagre, Frogs, and Sallad!

RECITATIVE.

A half-ſtarv'd Soldier, ſhirtleſs, pale, and lean,
Who ſuch a Sight before had never ſeen,
Like *Garrick*'s frighted *Hamlet*, gaping ſtood,
And gaz'd with Wonder on the *Britiſh* Food.
His Morning's Meſs forſook the friendly Bowl,
And in ſmall Streams along the Pavement ſtole;
He heav'd a ſigh, which gave his Heart Relief,
And then in plaintive Tone declared his Grief.

AIR.

Focie's Minuet.

Ah ſacré Dieu! 'vat do I ſee yonder
Dat looks ſo tempting, red and white?

Begar I ſee it is the *Roaſt Beef* from *Londre*:
O grant to me one letel Bite.

But to my Guts if you give no heeding,
And cruel Pate dis Boon denies,
In kind Compaſſion to my Pleading,
Return, and let me ſtudi my Eyes.

RECITATIVE.

His fellow Guard, of right *Hibernian* Clay,
Whoſe brazen Front, his Country did betray,
From *Tyburn*'s fatal Tree had hither fled,
By honeſt Means to get his daily Bread;
Soon as the well-known Project he eſpy'd,
In blubbering Accents dolefully he cry'd:

AIR.

Ellen a Roon, &c.

Sweet *Beef*, that now cauſes my Stomach to riſe,
Sweet *Beef*, that now cauſes my Stomach to riſe,
So taking thy Sight is,
My Joy, that to light is,
To view thee, by Pailfuls runs out at my Eyes.
While here I remain, my Life's not worth a Farthing,
While here I remain, my Life's not worth a Farthing.
Ah! hard-hearted *Lewy*,
Why did I come to ye,
The Gallows, more kind, would have ſav'd me from ſtarving.

RECITATIVE.

Upon the Ground hard by, poor *Sawney* ſate,
Who fed his Noſe, and ſcratch'd his ruddy Pate;
But when *Old England*'s Bulwark he deſcry'd,
His dear-lov'd Mull, alas! was thrown aſide.
With lifted Hands, he bleſt his native Place,
Then ſcrubb'd himſelf, and thus bewail'd his Caſe:

AIR.

The Broom of Cowdenknows, &c.

How hard, O *Sawney!* is thy Lot,
Who was ſo blyth of late,
To ſee ſuch Meat as can't be got,
When Hunger is ſo great!

O the *Beef!* the bonny bonny Beef!
When roaſted nice and brown,
I wiſh I had a ſlice of thee;
How ſweet it would gang down!

Ah, *Charley!* hadſt thou not been ſeen,
This ne'er had hapt to me:
I would the De'el had pickt mine Ey'n
Ere I had gang'd with thee.
O the *Beef! &c.*

RECITATIVE.

But ſee! my Muſe to *England* takes her flight,
Where *Health* and *Plenty* chearfully unite:
Where ſmiling *Freedom* guards *Great George*'s Throne,
And Chains, and Racks, and Tortures are not known:
Whoſe *Fame* ſuperior Bards have often wrote,——
An ancient Fable give me Leave to quote:

AIR.

The Roaſt Beef of Old England.

At once on a Time a young Frog, pert and vain,
Beheld a large Ox grazing on the wide Plain,
He bawled his Size he could quickly attain,
Oh! the *Roaſt Beef, &c.*

Then eagerly ſtretching his weak little Frame,
Mamma, who ſtood by, like a knowing old Dame,
Cry'd, "Son to attempt it you're greatly to blame."
Oh! the *Roaſt Beef, &c.*

But, deaf to Advice, he for Glory did thirſt,
An Effort he ventur'd, more ſtrong than the firſt,
Till ſwelling and ſtraining too hard made him burſt.
Oh! the *Roaſt Beef, &c.*

Then *Britons* be valiant, the moral is clear:
The Ox is *Old England*, the Frog is *Monſieur*,
Whoſe Puffs and Bravadoes we need not never fear.
Oh! the *Roaſt Beef, &c.*

For while by our Commerce and arts we are able,
To ſee the brave Ox ſmoaking hot on our Table,
The *French* muſt e'en croak like the Frog in the Fable.
Oh! the *Roaſt Beef, &c.*

LONDON: Printed for W. TRINGHAM, under the *North Piazza* of the *Royal Exchange*, in *Threadneedle-Street*.

PLATE 1.7 : Broadside-cantata with recitative and five airs.
The Roast Beef of Old England. Des: anon. After the painting and print by William
Hogarth. (1697–1764). Etching, engraving and letterpress. Printed for W. Tringham
under the North Piazza of the Royal Exchange in Threadneedle Street,
London c.1759? 42.8 x 26.9. 25949. This is one of at least two editions of a
broadside cantata based around the popular song *The Roast Beef of Old England*.
It capitalised on Hogarth's well-known painting of 1748 and subsequent print:
The Gate of Calais, or The Roast Beef of Old England. (cf. Paulson (1989) cat. 180).

PLATE 1.8.a : Probable frontispiece. *Clementi & Co's Edition of Handel's Songs.* Des: G.B. Cipriani (1727–1785). Ex: Francesco Bartolozzi R.A.(1727–1815). Etching and Stipple engraving. Pub: the composer, Muzio Clementi. c.1803–1807. Sight-size: 34.5 x 27.2. 29599.K. Bartolozzi arrived in England in 1764 already possessing a reputation for his fine classical formulations and mastery of the stipple technique, replacing the simple linear hatching of engraving with dots and stars to achieve soft tonal renderings. Working frequently to the drawings of his one-time pupil Cipriani, Bartolozzi produced an estimated 2,500 plates including many music title pages and benefit tickets for musical friends and performers. Cipriani's layouts and Bartolozzi's technique recall Parisian music-titles of the 1730s engraved by Simon Henri Thomassin (1687–1741) after designs by Nicolas Lancret (1690–1745) and by Jacques Philippe Lebas (1707–1783). (See Fraenkel, G. S. (1968) plates 126 and 127).

PLATE 1.8.b : Periodical title page.
Loder's Edition of Handel's Songs.
Des. & ex: Barrett & Barrif, 84, Dean St., Soho. Etching and stipple. Pub, printed & sold by John David Loder, Bath. (1793–1846). c.1820. Plate-mark: 27.7 x 20.3. E. 2642–1921.
Published for the amateur market in the fashionable city of Bath in single numbers as keyboard arrangements of Handel's popular songs. The page design presumably remained constant, distinguished only by ink numbering added at the warehouse or shop.

PLATE 1.9 : A broadside and four broadside–ballads.

Sale of A Wife. Des: anon. English. Woodcut and letterpress.
Pr: M'Cernack. Nineteenth century. 30.3 x 18.4. E. 860–1954.
Probably a revivalist example of the black-letter form
of broadside recounting the traditional tale of wife selling,
which is, in this instance, accompanied by *The Wedding Song*.

The Hunting of Chevy-Chace. 40 verses. Des: anon. English. Woodcut and letterpress.
Early-eighteenth century. 25.5 x 35.2. E. 298–1947. Registered in 1642,
this ballad and its tune were popular for many generations.

The Mistletoe Bough and *The Land*. Des: anon.
Wood-engraving and letterpress. Pub. & Pr. J. Catnach
(1792–1841), London. c.1820s–'30s. 23.5 x 14.5. E. 1326–1990.
It was a commonplace to see a well-known song such as
The Mistletoe Bough (here with a short account of its
tragic theme), paired with a new composition.
Printed in a single operation, the sheet
could be sold complete or cut into slips.

Still I Love Thee and *Please Give me a Penny Sir*.
Des: anon. Wood-engraving and letterpress.
Pub. & pr: W.S. Fortey (d.1901), by steam press,
London. c.1848 or later. 24.6 x 18.8. E. 1325–1990.
Much of Fortey's stock had at one time
belonged to Pitts, Catnach and successors.

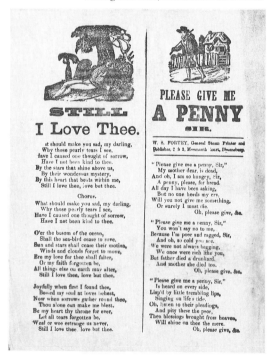

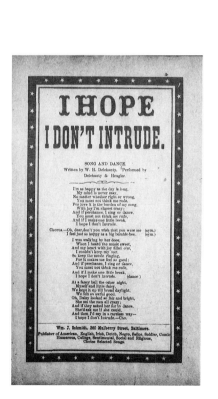

I Hope I Don't Intrude. A song and dance written by Delahanty and
performed by Delahanty and Hengler. Des: anon. Letterpress.
Pub: William Schmidt, Baltimore. Ninteenth century. 23.5 x 14.5.
E. 1327–1990. Copy states that American, English, Irish, Dutch,
Negro, sailor, soldier, comic, humorous, college, sentimental,
social and religious '*choice selected songs*' are available.
Note the border of American State stars.

**PLATE 1.10.a : Broadside-ballad
and title page.** *Peter Snout*. Des. & ex:
George Cruikshank (1792–1878). Hand-coloured
etching and letterpress. Pub: J. Whittle &
R.H. Laurie,
No. 53, Fleet Street, London. 1816. 30.2 x 23.8
9477.F. Copy states that this was
*'sung with universal Applause by
Mr. Sloman and Mr. Munden'*.

1.10.b : Title page. *Four New Comic Songs
"La Bagatelle"*. Composed by G. Cooke.
Illus: Cruikshank. Hand-coloured etching.
Pub: Leader & Cock, 63 New Bond Street,
corner of Brook St. n.d. 35.2 x 25.9. 9433.3.
Copy states sheets are: Plain 5s/- , Coloured 6/-.
Note Cruikshank's 'musical' signature.

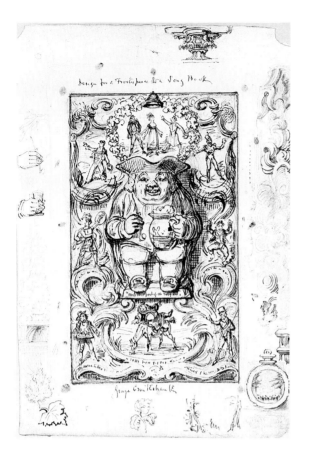

1.11.a : Design for a song-book frontispiece.
The Universal Songster. Signed George Cruikshank.
Pencil, pen and ink. c.1825. 27.6 x 19.2. 9557.A.
A working drawing for the frontispiece to
The Universal Songster, discarded after just a few
copies were issued. (See Cohn (1924) cat. 820).

1.11.b : Song-book frontispiece. Frontispiece to the first
volume of *The Universal Songster.* Des. & ex: George
Cruikshank. Etched on steel. Pub: John Fairburn,
Broadway Ludgate Hill. June 11th 1825. 30.2 x 21.5. 9561.2.
This is the version finally selected to front the work.
The copy claims that the Universal Songster's three volumes
form: *'…the most complete, extensive and valuable
collection of ancient and modern songs in the English
language…'* The volumes include three etched frontispieces
by Cruikshank and 84 wood-engravings, of which 24 are
after Cruikshank, and 57 after his brother Robert.

PLATE 1.12.a : Broadsheet. *The 'Derby' Monster Songster!* Des: anon. Wood-engraving and letterpress. Pub: J.T. Wood, The Strand. 1865. 83.3 x 54.5 (folded to: 43.4 x 27.8cm). E. 1771–1990. 116 songs fronted by a three-block wood-engraving of crowds at the Epsom Derby in the manner of Frith's oil painting, *Derby Day* (1858). The sheet carries the names of song-writers, composers, singers and music publishers together with this warning: *'Legal proceedings will be taken against song-book publishers and others printing any of the copyright songs contained in this book.'*

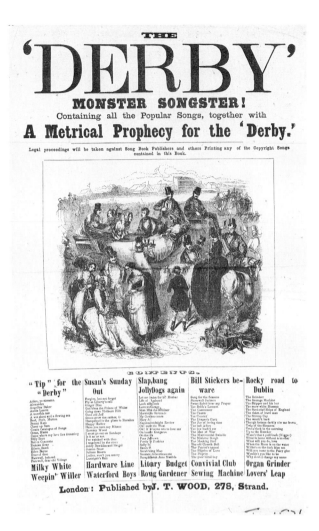

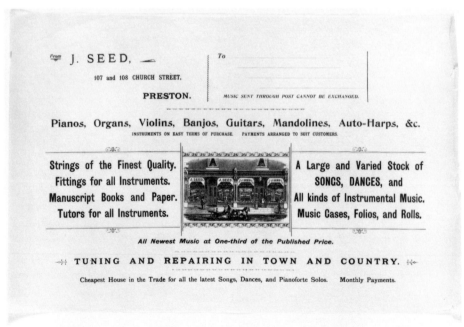

PLATE 1.12.b : Wrapping for song-sheets distributed by post. J. Seed Piano and Organ Rooms, Preston. Des: anon. Line-block and letterpress on waterproof paper. c.1885. 29.8 x 46.7. E. 1329–1990. This sheet serves as a trade-card and imparts general merchandising information.

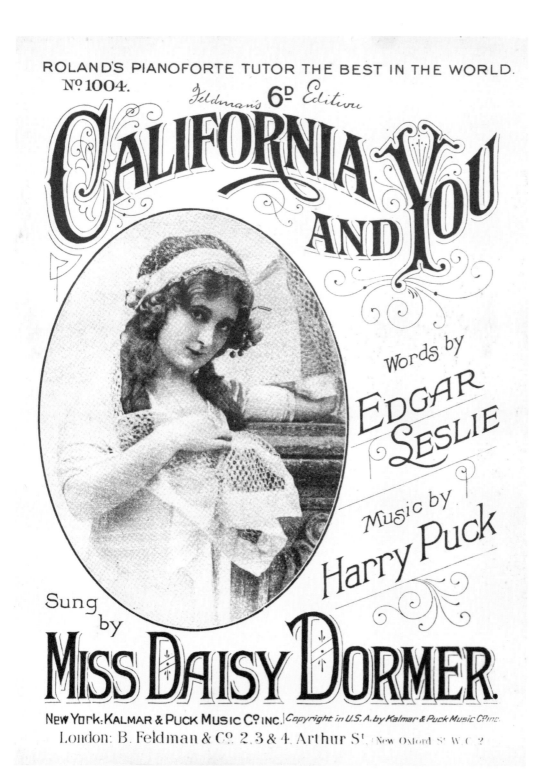

PLATE 1.13 : Song-sheet. *California and You.* sung by Miss Daisy Dormer. One of Bert Feldman's 6d. editions. Des: anon. Offset lithography. Pub: Kalmar & Puck Music Co. Inc., New York and B. Feldman & Co. London. 1914. Folded to: 35.6 x 26.5. E. 1753–1990. Feldman specialised in heavily promoted, cheap editions of popular American and British songs performed by popular artists, photos of whom would feature in decorous designs such as this. To foster amateur musicianship and stimulate sales, a photograph of Feldman appears on the back of this sheet to endorse a piano tutor-book.

PLATE 1.14.a : Song-sheet.
The Dark Town Strutter's Ball. (The musical story
of the Dolly Sisters, a Twentieth Century Fox film.)
Des: anon. Offset lithography.
Pub: Leo Feist Inc., New York and Francis, Day & Hunter,
London. 1945. Folded to: 27.8 x 21.6. E. 1750–1990.
Typical of its kind, this sheet has ukulele chord shapes,
Sol-Fa markings and standard chord abbreviations within to
accompany the piano arrangement.

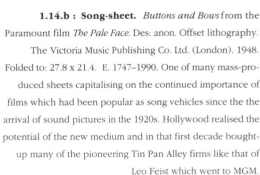

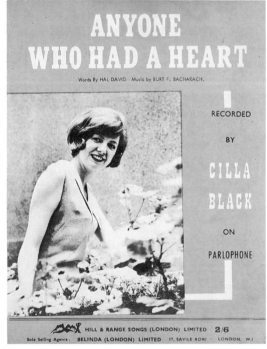

1.14.b : Song-sheet. *Buttons and Bows* from the
Paramount film *The Pale Face*. Des: anon. Offset lithography.
The Victoria Music Publishing Co. Ltd. (London). 1948.
Folded to: 27.8 x 21.4. E. 1747–1990. One of many mass-produced sheets capitalising on the continued importance of
films which had been popular as song vehicles since the the
arrival of sound pictures in the 1920s. Hollywood realised the
potential of the new medium and in that first decade bought-
up many of the pioneering Tin Pan Alley firms like that of
Leo Feist which went to MGM.

1.14.c : Song-sheet. *Anyone Who had a Heart*.
Recorded by Cilla Black on Parlophone.
Offset lithography. Pub: Hill & Range Songs
(London) Ltd. 1963. Folded to: 28.0 x 21
E.1745–1990. Prosaic 'identification' photo-portraits
of performers like these whose antecedents lie on
sheets of earlier centuries are a stock music business
promotional device still very much in evidence
in the last decade of this century.

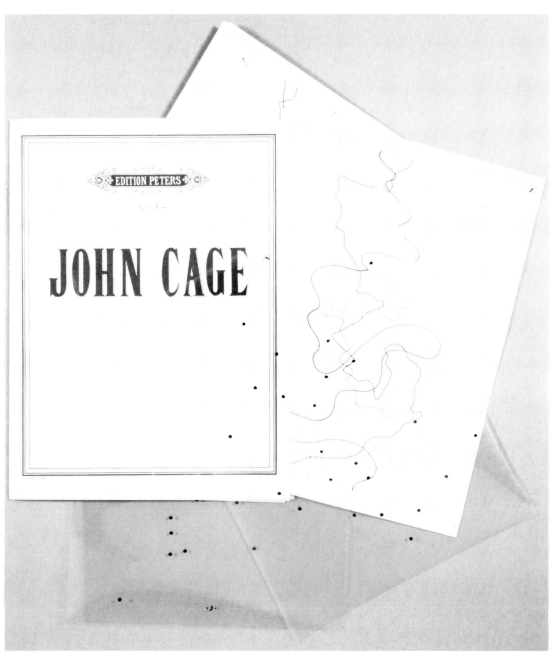

PLATE 1.15.a : Score. *Fontana Mix.* John Cage (b.1912). Des: Cage. Offset lithography and printed acetate sheets. 1958. 29.7 x 22.7. V&A Museum, National Art Library, C. 25401.

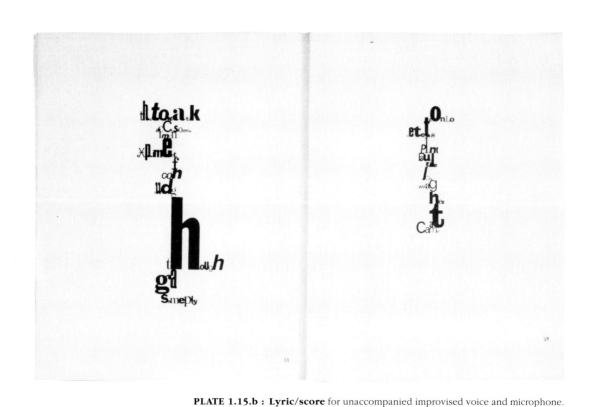

PLATE 1.15.b : Lyric/score for unaccompanied improvised voice and microphone.
Sixty-Two Mesostics Re Merce Cunningham. Conceived by John Cage. Offset lithography.
1971. Opens to: 36.9 x 58.0. V&A Museum, National Art Library, C. 25562.
The text, using 750 letterset type-faces is taken from *Changes: Notes on Choreography by Merce
Cunningham*, and is determined by *I Ching*. Cage notes: *'...to raise language's temperature we not only
remove syntax: we give each letter undivided attention setting it in unique face and size: to read
becomes the verb to sing.'* The notational experiments of 'serious' composers like Cage have created
new relationships between composition, improvisation and graphics on paper. These have failed to
stimulate parallel advances in the fields of music publishing where familiarity and accessibility for the
non-specialist are regarded as necessary components in 'popular' scores. This attitude overlooks the
amateur's prior knowledge of a piece gleaned from recordings. Stravinsky indeed stated that
recordings of his work could subsist as aural guides to future performance. Instances of some popular
song-books where lyric and scores are treated more imaginatively than in most cases are
The Second Clash Song-book, illustrated by Derek Boshier, *Kings* for Adam and the Ants (1981)
and song-books designed by Assorted Images for The Buzzcocks.

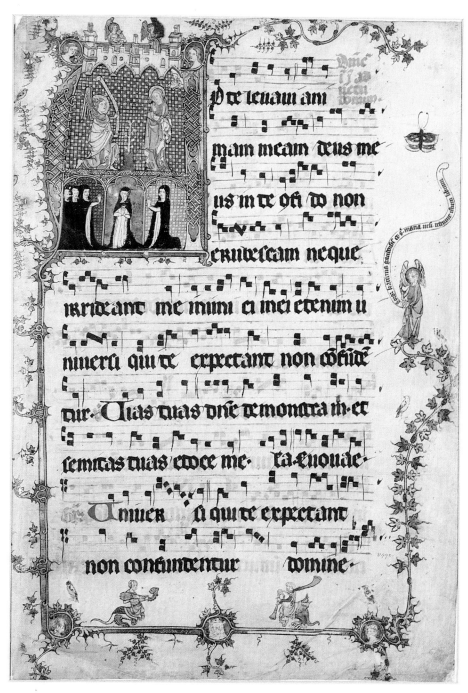

PLATE 1.16 : Opening leaf of a gradual. *1st Sunday in Advent.*
Des: anon. Netherlandish illuminated manuscript on parchment. c.1330.
47.0 x 32.2. 8992. The Latin inscription on the scroll held by the angel on the
right states that it was donated to the Dominican Nunnery by Sister Katerina
of Gouda and Sister Mari Ursi. A manuscript of this quality would be
executed by the best scribes and illuminators (religious or secular) available
at this date. (Note the portative organ, rebec, gittern and bagpipes
of which the last three are secular instruments).

PLATE 1.17.a : Song-sheet.
I Wait to Hear Thy Sweet Good Night!
Jenny Lind's Good Night. Des: anon.
Colour lithography. Pub: Hopwood & Crew,
London. Pr: Stannard & Dixon. 1840s.
31.5 x 25.0. E. 2616–1921.

1.17.b : Song-sheet. *La Figlia Del Regimento.*
Des: W. Taft. Colour lithography. Pub: C. J. Jeffreys.
'Printed in colours by W. Stannard.' c.1848.
34.7 x 24.3. E. 794–1947. The copy states that
Mad'le Jenny Lind sings the Italian and Miss Rebecca
Isaacs the English version. The price of the sheet
being 2/-, or 2/6 in colours. Jenny Lind,
the so-called Swedish Nightingale was one
of the first performers to attain 'star' status
both here and in the United States as a result
of her talent and determined
publicity campaigns.

PLATE 1.18.a : Song-sheet. *Garage.*
Des: Man Ray (1890–1977). Ex: Marcel-Louis
Baugniet (b.1896). Line-block and lithography.
'Grav. et imp. J. De Vleeschouwer,
*Evere-Bruxelles.'.*Pub: Edition Music, 25,
Boulevard Bischoffsheim Bruxelles.
An edition of five hundred. c.1926. Folded to:
34.6 x 26.8. E. 325–1984. *Garage* is a Philippe
Soupault poem set to music by E. L. T. Mesens
for which Ray was asked to design a cover.
Such knowing, cross-media confections
which are at one remove from the realm of
commercial production were common in
the early twentieth century.

PLATE 1.18.b : Song-book. *Robbins' No. 1 Frank*
Sinatra Album of Hit Songs from his LP Records.
Des: anon. Offset lithography. Pub: Robbins Music
Corp. Ltd. c.1956. 27.6 x 21.5 E. 1759–1990. The
arrival of the LP in the late 1940s gave the music
business a new product which was soon to rival the
cinema in appeal and profit. This song-book attests
a transitional phase in that shift of interest.
It contains eight songs supported by three black and
white movie stills of Sinatra. The back of
the song-book advertises volume two.

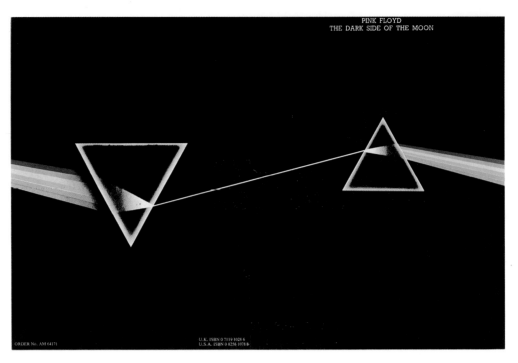

PLATE 1.19.a : Song-book. *The Dark Side of the Moon*. Pink Floyd (Back and front).
Des: Hipgnosis (Storm Thorgerson, b.1944 with Aubery Powell) and George Hardy NTA. Offset lithography.
Pub: Pink Floyd Music Publishers Ltd. London. Pr: Vicks Lithograph and Printing Corporation. USA.
LP released March 1973. 30:1 x 44.6. Private Collection.
The prism and spectrum motif of the gatefold LP sleeve reappears, communicating in an instant,
its relationship to the highly-successful recording. The Song arrangements are supported by photographs
of Pink Floyd in concert, interviews with band members and the all-important discography.

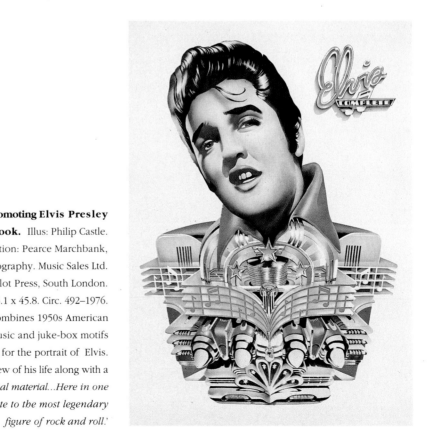

PLATE 1.19.b : Poster promoting Elvis Presley
song-book. Illus: Philip Castle.
(Book's art direction: Pearce Marchbank,
des: Paul May). Offset lithography. Music Sales Ltd.
Pr: Camelot Press, South London.
1976. 63.1 x 45.8. Circ. 492–1976.
Castle's airbrush design combines 1950s American
car components with music and juke-box motifs
which serve as a 'period' foil for the portrait of Elvis.
The book contains a review of his life along with a
*unique collection of visual material...Here in one
book, the greatest tribute to the most legendary
figure of rock and roll.'*

PLATE 1.20 : Song-book. *The Ian Dury Songbook.* Illus: Barney Bubbles (real name Colin Fucher, 1942–1983).
Offset lithography. Pr: West Central Printing Co. Ltd., London. 30.2 x 23.0. E.1308–1990. The removable blue sticker is
a precautionary addition more often found on record sleeves when it is thought necessary to highlight the 'hits' within,
or override adventurous artwork which, it is feared, may fail to apprise consumers of the contents.
The illustrations within are in the same, idiosyncratic pink and black mode.
This song-book stand alongside the second song-book of The Clash (1979) by Derek Boshier (b. 1937)
in terms of overt graphic waywardness within the confines of a normally, well-prescribed commodity formula.

PLATE 1.21.a : Song-book. *Miss Saigon.*
Des: Dewynters PLC, London.
Offset lithography. Pub: Wise Publications.
30.4 x 22. 8. Private collection.
The back cover carries portraits of the musical's
composer and lyricist, together with press
comments about the stage show. There is also
copy promoting The original London cast album
of *Miss Saigon* in which the CD, double LP and
double-play cassette catalogue numbers are given.

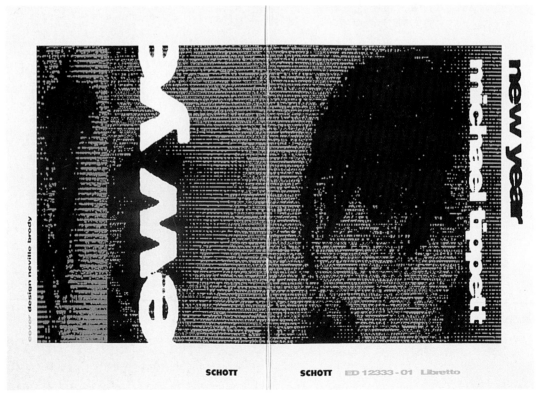

PLATE 1.21.b : Opera vocal score. *New Year*, Sir Michael Tippett. Des: Neville Brody. (b.1957).
Offset lithography. Pub: Schott & Co. 1989. Opens to 30.5 x 46.6.

SELLING THE
MUSICAL SPECTACLE

POSTERS, HANDBILLS
AND TICKETS

*'They who advertise the Comedie and the Opéra
never set foot in them. When they've put the
writing perpendicular to the street and its quite
straight, they contemplate it with an air of
satisfaction and go...'*

An extract from Mercier's eighteenth century
History of Paris
Cited Weill, A. (1985) p.14.

49

SELLING THE MUSICAL SPECTACLE
POSTERS, HANDBILLS AND TICKETS

Posters, Handbills and Tickets: Functions and Forms.

Just as printed lyrics and music took learned and courtly forms of music into the domestic setting and tavern, so posters, press advertisements and ticket outlets drew paying, appreciative masses out of the house, across the noisy street and into public venues to hear that same music professionally performed.

Graphics for musical spectacles were and continue to be used to signify the presence, promote the imminent occurrence and encapsulate the essence of a commodified 'product': a social and aesthetic spectacle to *see* and music to hear, enjoy, discuss, dance, romance or dine to in the company of peers and superiors.[1]

The graphics surveyed here are those for festivals, concerts and dances. Those promoting radio, television and video are omitted on the grounds that they are essentially geared to solitary domestic consumption, an experience which is at one remove from the adrenaline-fed social discourse of the live musical spectacle.

This sphere of the music business has become, in the second-half of the twentieth century, the least lucrative means of song-selling and is, in its simplest un-recorded forms, closest to the immaterial, time-based commodity described in the introduction. The unique event does of course attract press, radio and television interest but it is essentially a transitory, cultural commodity repeatable and saleable only in a recorded form. For many in the music business today, the musical spectacle is, at best, a merchandiser's pitch and a marketing lever for record sales.

Posters. Posters have usually been produced to occupy fixed sites (chiefly exterior ones), with the aim of communicating essential information by catching the eye of passers by on foot or in cars, buses and trains.

Each new musical spectacle is a new 'product' demanding fresh, unambiguous graphic treatment in order to rival other posters on the hoardings which are also competing for attention. Posters linked to the music business are 'silent' sheets which must invoke the sounds of the spectacle with words, symbols and imagery. These often consist of simple representations of featured singers, dancers, instruments or other stock musical images but some designers in this area have risen above the cliché and have generated some of the most inventive poster designs to be seen in any period.

The street poster frequently differs considerably from related press advertisements. It is invariably larger, and it is usually dominated by distinguished forms and colours; the text-message is also less complex and more prominent. Posters are undoubtedly for the eyes, press advertisements are for the brain. With the poster, intellectual cognition is preceded by instinctive, nonconscious engagement. The aim is to communicate the imminent advent of a spectacle to an individual who may then consult the press for further details or ask the the venue or agent cited in the poster for further information. Venue details, prices, dates and times tend to sit on the poster in a detached, less intense manner isolated graphically and spatially from the primary image and major typographical line.

2.10.a,b

There are of course exceptions where surfaces are crowded with a dozen or more events and dense text which can only be read slowly by an individual who has time to wade through a fair amount of printed information as they perhaps wait for a bus or train.[2]

Since the inception of the 'art poster' in the late-nineteenth century, poster sheets have also functioned as something more than transmitters of ephemeral messages. They have become objects to collect as souvenirs and display as works of art.[3] Rather like today's rock group world-tour t-shirt and glossy souvenir programme, the poster has become, in its own right, a saleable commodity of lasting worth for consumers which has a post-event sales life of months or years.[4]

Posters in the role of 'stand-alone', souvenir merchandise are ultimately related to the sixteenth and seventeenth-century Italian *descrizioni*: festival-books and programmes (often complete with a libretto), which recorded the wedding celebrations of ruling families and other high-profile ceremonies.[5]

Handbills, leaflets and Flyers. Handbills are conceived as small, 'mobile' posters with print on one or both sides. They display imagery and information seen on associated press advertisements and posters and often carry extra details on performers and the pieces to be played. They are distributed by hand in the street or offered from fixed points in venue foyers and are designed to stay with the potential ticket buyer acting as visual prompts. Similar to the handbill is the leaflet: a folded sheet carrying the same forms and messages as posters and handbills, but which may also subsist as a more extensive guide to a series of concerts or festival events. Occasionally this information is also presented as a booklet with small format sheets folded as a book into pages and stapled together to form durable informational guides to a string of associated musical spectacles.

Flyers are the modern-day equivalents of the traditional handbill: low-cost, one-sided sheets of paper or card confirming word-of-mouth, press, radio or television announcements to individuals known to frequent a particular locale and who are regarded by promoters and the flyer distributors as potential audience members. Conveying primary information only, flyers may also function as complimentary tickets or offer price reductions to the bearer on entry. They are frequently picked-up in record stores by young concert and dance goers or handed-out only a few days, hours or even minutes before the start of an event. They range from the simple photocopy to an elaborately designed and coloured sheet designed to capture the attentions of passers-by.

Tickets and Programmes. Admission tickets function in this field as tangible, attractive receipts and prompts which confer upon holders the right to attend the designated performance. Since the nineteenth century, tickets have listed performance dates, times, details of seat numbers, venue entrances, suitable modes of transport and availability of printed lyrics. Today they also list performer and promoter details and will often carry a promotional message about an associated record release. Warnings about 'pirate' merchandise are to be found on most tickets for mass-market events as are standard restrictions on photography and recording together with the rights of

event organisers to film the audience during the performance.

2.11.a

Prosaic typography so often suffices to convey much of the vital ticket information outlined here, yet since the eighteenth century, promoters have employed designers to create attractive, distinctive imagery or adapt designs, familiar logotypes or passe-partout frames for tickets as suitable foils for manuscript or letterpress concert details. Well-designed tickets can, like posters, convey an impression of the impending concert as envisaged by the promoters which might be a grand, restrained, boisterous, revivalist or avant-garde event. Once a consumer likes and learns to recognise the projected image of a particular venue or performer it is very likely that they will choose to 'buy' a similarly 'commodified' spectacle in the future.

Programmes impart performance particulars as well as information on forthcoming associated events. They frequently carry advertisements for recordings, details on sponsorship and advertisements for associated consumer durables such as radiograms and pianos. They often also carry portraits and biographies of featured performers so that like posters, handbills, flyers and tickets, they can help establish character profiles for the musicians and venues.

2.8.b
2.9.a

Promoting Spectacles before 1690.

Before the eighteenth century, ordered musical performances were sacred or civil, non-commercial events for audiences in church, in the *piazza*, town square, great hall, private chapel, tavern or court. Frequency and determination of the form of these events was dominated by the religious calendar and the social activities of ruling orders. The music provided by resident choristers, itinerant troubadours, court retainers and waits followed precedent and was enlivened by innovative theatrical spectacles. It was the symbolism of these events as much as the music itself which was being presented for free 'consumption'.

The nature of performance promotion is difficult to assess in this era but there was probably little reliance on paper and ink, communication surrounding a forthcoming, non-annual event being verbal.

Amongst the earliest forms of pre-planned musical spectacles for audiences out-numbering musicians were the festivals of Italy, particularly the Florentine shows geared to honour the ruling Medici family and the nascent operatic spectacles in the *palazzi* of Venice and Rome. These lively combinations of rehearsed secular music, choreography and drama crossed the Alps in the mid-seventeenth century and eventually inspired the court entertainments of Louis XIII and Louis XIV and the court masques of the Stuarts. Running parallel to Britain's courtly events were straight dramatic performances for paying audiences enhanced with music from off-stage musicians.

In 1642, under the Commonwealth, English theatres were closed forcing their musicians to join former court musicians in seeking alternative employment in more modest, and informal venues, which in time fostered a broad taste for learned music. Restoration of the monarchy in 1660 led inevitably to a revival of court entertainments coinciding with the arrival of baroque musical forms from Italy and France. To satisfy general public demand across Europe for more music, public concerts surfaced, notably in Hamburg in the 1660s. In England in the 1670s, John Banister (c.1625–79), leader of the royal string orchestra, began to hold concerts in the music room of his Whitefriars house which had been designed to accommodate paying audiences while imitating a tavern music-room. These concerts were often daily events and were advertised in the press and in handbills given out in inns and coffee-houses; they were also posted through the doors of the wealthy in an early instance of direct marketing. The information on them was limited to performers: already promoters realised that personalities exerted more allure than the often unfamiliar, 'faceless' composition.[6]

The Spectacle c.1690–c.1790

The discrete commercial spectacle continued to prosper in eighteenth century Europe, (most notably in London, Paris and Vienna), as the aspiring merchant classes with time and money sought to patronise musical events in emulation of the aristocracy. Wide-spread musical interest in London was fuelled by the arrival of new generations of Continental performers and composers supported in their professions by the capital's high number of organised musical events and considerable opportunities for teaching. Travel abroad extended British musical tastes, while commerce at home increased the amount of dis-

posable income which might be spent on entertainment. In the seventeenth century, people had performed music at home as accomplished instrumentalists, in the eighteenth century many elected to be gauche, concert-going amateurs leaving the grind of practice and formal performance to the professional.[7]

In spite of the increasing 'exclusivity' of venues and the more precise targetting of particular social groups, music continued to draw upon all manner of sources and appeal to all tastes, high and low. As Leppert writes:

> Commerce as such was potentially levelling, nothing mattered so much as one's ability to pay. Hence all classes of English society might attend the theatre or even the opera, both of which were highly popular forms of general entertainment.[8]

Italian opera, never entirely at home in England, was never the less nurtured by Purcell and Handel with both using London's theatres as settings for elaborate operatic conceits. Handel's opera *Rinaldo*, was performed in 1711 and received much acclaim from his aristocratic followers but it fared less well with the more insular concert patron schooled in non-musical English drama. To try and make opera more palatable, word-books were printed for English audiences. Issued in support of *Rinaldo* was a 20.2 x 12.9 cm word-book containing the Italian libretto and an English translation printed by the Queen's Theatre printer, Thomas Howlatt. This 1711 edition was followed by subsequent editions in the following decades.

A key aspect of the eighteenth-century musical scene was the fashionable Vauxhall Gardens. Originally opened as the New Spring Gardens they were relaunched after The Restoration by the entrepreneur, Jonathan Tyers, (d.1767) who provided elegant walks, temples and water-courses in the latest styles to be enjoyed along with the pleasures of eating, drinking and listening to the music of the central concert stand. The gardens were largely self-promoting, requiring the minimum amount of printed publicity. It is interesting to note, however, that they were responsible for encouraging the production and sale of many half-sheets capitalising on the cachet conferred by a performance in the gardens. Although its music was largely an accompaniment to society gatherings it did serve at least once as a more formal venue when in 1749 Handel staged a rehearsal in the Gardens for his *Music for Royal Fireworks*. He attracted twelve thousand spectators, each paying a two shillings and sixpence entry fee.

What really excited insular taste was *The Beggar's Opera* (first performed 1728) written by John Gay (1685–1732), a show laced with sharp wit and popular English song. Music *per se* in the theatre gained more ground following the 1737 licensing act which confined straight drama to certain London stages. Provincial music clubs in places like Norwich, Bristol and Birmingham together with the all-pervasive and very fashionable catch and glee clubs further prepared the ground for ambitious civic festivals like that in Birmingham in 1768 and Norwich in 1770.[9] Composers also stimulated the burgeoning concert scene with Carl Friedrich Abel (1723–87) and Johann Christian Bach (1735–82) organising and performing at frequent subscription concerts between 1765 and 1781.[10]

2.4

In North America there were, from the 1720s until after the Revolution, many European musicians travelling to and settling in the Eastern States. Their collective presence encouraged musical activity in Philadelphia, New York and Boston. Events in America tended to echo the popular forms seen in Europe, (formal concerts in America at this time were few) with many taking-part in locally-generated dances and concerts served by hybrid musical works possessing sacred and folk elements. In America, commercial musical promotion remained centred on the newspaper well into the next century as theatre-bills and handbills which worked so well in an increasingly urbanised Europe,were less effective across the wide-open lands of the New World.

Promotional Graphics in Eighteenth Century London. London's complex musical life received a good deal of concise publicity in the four newspapers and numerous periodicals and journals read widely in the homes, taverns and coffee-houses of the 1760s. As with later seventeenth-century concert advertisements, those of the eighteenth century advanced the name of a personality. An example that printed in 1792 to advertise a season of concerts at Hanover Square presided over by Johann Peter Salomon (1745–1815). The copy addressed nobility and gentry, recalled the spectacular concerts of the previous year, noted the expected presence of '*Mr. Haydn*', named the soloists and for good measure announced that the orchestra would be augmented to offer variety.[11]

Street advertisements took the form of painted theatre name-boards, canvases or banners executed by in-house designers which might stay fixed to venue-facades for several seasons. Details of changing programmes and performers were conveyed by letterpress theatre-bills which could be pasted-up on boards and walls at the venue itself and, more importantly, elsewhere within the locality. A 1783 watercolour of The Queen's Theatre (now in the Guildhall Library), shows four bills posted on to its facade proclaiming forthcoming events. Three are headed with the Royal Coat of Arms which also appear on a theatre-bill for a performance of *The Beggar's Opera* at the Theatre Royal, seen in Hogarth's engraving of *The Enraged Musician* (1741), which is incidentally more an iconographical construct than a straight depiction of London musical life. The Royal Coat of Arms headpiece is still used today on the printed literature of The Royal Opera House.[12]

These theatre-bills were printed in black ink and had formats delimited partly by the size of the hand-made paper and partly by the constraints of the printer's wooden, hand-operated press. In Paris, the royal theatres distinguished their posters by printing them on a selection of coloured papers. It is likely that all these unadorned typographical announcements, would have been the preserve of local jobbing printers. Intaglio printing rarely, if ever featured in bills and posters of this date.

For outstanding artistic contributions to the business of selling live music at this time, one has to turn to ticket design. The dominance of the small-format, monochromatic letterpress theatre-bill was only challenged in the mid-nineteenth century by the coming of colour lithography and large, mechanised presses.

Admission Tickets and Programmes in the Eighteenth Century. All eighteenth-century tickets that survive are intaglio prints though promoters of annual events such as the Vauxhall season issued durable ticket tokens of metal to seasonal subscribers.

Francesco Bartolozzi RA (1727–1815), engraved some 40 or more distinctive and fine benefit admission tickets after designs by Giovanni Battista Cipriani (1727–85), during their time together in London. Although only slight beside his more substantial stipple prints, it is likely that his tickets were to be seen framed on the walls of those seeking to decorate their homes with a print by one of the most fashionable engravers of the day. From the first, a Bartolozzi ticket was a highly prized possession with many being salvaged by 'connoisseurs' from doormen at the end of a concert. Indeed Bartolozzi himself hung proofs of his tickets on his own walls. The decorative nature of tickets in general was acknowledged by printers who used not only black but the then fashionable sanguine and blue inks.[13]

2.3

The V&A Museum holds a ticket executed in 1808 by Niccolo Schiavonetti Junior (1771–1813) for the Great Concert Room in the King's Theatre Haymarket which is lettered thus: *'NB this check will admit the subscriber without the print'*. This option offered holders the chance to reduce the size of the unwieldy sheet and preserve the image at home.[14]

2.4

An etched and engraved frontispiece to Leveridge's 1727 *Collection of Songs* by the young Hogarth, (it comprised two volumes sold by subscription promoted in the press) appears to have been reworked in 1750 to serve as a benefit ticket for the opera singer, Signor Laschi, performing at the King's Theatre Haymarket.[15]

Economies in ticket production of a similar kind are seen in a fine stipple engraved admission ticket for the Theatre Royal, Haymarket which has lettering stating that an oratorio will be performed and that boxes are 5s. This elaborate design leaves blank spaces for the name of the oratorio and the day of performance to be added by hand at the point of sale.[16]

When opera programmes in the eighteenth century were not substantial word-books, they were usually single-sheet letterpress handbills carrying plot summaries and many of the details seen on larger theatre-bills. Programmes were sold inside and outside theatres or given away with fruit bought before a performance. They may frequently have functioned as posters, being posted or pinned around the city or distributed within the locality and at music shop counters. The exact titles, key signatures and other analytical information which today is expected to be contained in an instrumental concert programme is, at this date, noticeably absent. A small, (c.10.0 x c.7.5cm) Philharmonic Society concert programme-card, issued as late as 1813, offers just two words to describe one of its items: *'Symphony Haydn'*. A handbill-programme for Haydn's benefit concert in May 1795 (now in a private collection), has been annotated by the original owner, who, alongside

the printed words *Military Symphony* has written the comment *'Grand but very noisy'*. Evidently in this case, the card served as a 'memo-pad' for a keen concert-goer.[17]

Selling the Spectacle. c.1790–1890.[18]

The picture at this date is one of ever-increasing mass-participation in communal music-making and concert-going stimulated by the urban influx of labouring classes demanding urban 'pop' entertainment at regular times of the day. Disposable incomes continued to rise while at the same time, tastes became increasingly more sophisticated and more learned because of the introduction of musical education at and beyond school. As a consequence, concert repertories were broadened, and an interest in early music was encouraged by such institutions as the Purcell Society founded in 1876. The notion of reviving and selling music of an earlier period emerges in the nineteenth century and has enormous implications for music as an autonomous, aesthetic commodity in later years.[19] By the nineteenth century, so many professional musicians were available to meet demands for performances in large urban centres that some of them used press advertisements for concerts as opportunities for flagrant self-promotion.

Music Hall. Parallel to the 'establishment' concert scene was that of the 'popular' concert found in smaller theatres, taverns and music halls and which played host to comics and acrobats as well as singers.

Beginning as venues for Saturday evening amateur performers and wishing to compete with the fading glories of Vauxhall and Ranelagh, such informal concert venues of the 1820s began to evolve and lay foundations for the professionally-organised supper rooms and music halls of the second-half of the century.

In spite of the improvisatory appearance of these function-room operations, they were run by professionals who were able to generate huge song-sheet sales as well as substantial profits from the sales of food and alcohol. Russell writes: *'Music hall was an industry capable of reacting in a sophisticated manner to changes in the market, and not a spontaneous popular creation.*[20] Owners of nineteenth-century music halls in the West End of London would pass a number of tickets on to the press in order to generate extra publicity – a practice still encountered today. Also exploiting the promotional opportunities of the benefit concerts tradition, music hall promoters would stage 'star benefit' nights, allowing audience fraternisation with the stars of the stage. Music halls were always carefully sited near a ready audience such as that living and working in the London docks. A good deal of local 'word of mouth' recommendation in these areas was enhanced with boldly-adorned hall facades proclaiming the names of the entertainers; regular regional coverage in the general press and in trade papers such as *The Era* (1838–1939) and *Entr'acte* (1869–1907) completed the promotional network. To bolster attendances, touring performers would themselves take out what were termed 'cards' in the press to advertise their unique presence at one venue or another.[21]

From 1900, British music publishers, imitating Tin Pan Alley's exploitation of the 'catchy chorus' in song-selling sent their new, chorus-dominated tunes out on to the commercially-orientated music hall circuits. The constant airing of a song and the 'joining-in' of an audience reading from cheaply-produced letterpress sheets on coloured paper did much to encourage sheet-music sales. In 1912, an illustration of the interior of The Hackney Empire was printed on the front of one of its own, rather grand 'in-house' song-sheets. This example came complete with a full musical arrangement and so served equally-well as a promotional vehicle for its publisher, Bert Feldman.

Jenny Lind and Barnum in America. In mid-nineteenth century America, European operatic composers and performers continued to hold sway on the musical stage with many touring the land to great acclaim.[22] In 1851 a French promoter took Jenny Lind (1820–87) on a massive tour of eighteen American cities, who gave a staggering thirty five performances in New York City alone. Her Madison concert tickets were in such demand that they were actually sold to the highest bidders at auction. Such an enthusiastic response must have been due in part to the advertising campaign organised by circus-promoter P. T. Barnum (1810–91). Barnum's large-scale advertising campaigns on the street had begun because of restrictions on display advertising in the press. He turned to a wood-engraver, Edward Purcell, who cut large portraits on pine planks rather than on the conventional small boxwood end-grain blocks, making large-format posters to promote his American Museum which hosted circus and variety performances. The museum itself was decorated with paintings of animals and with flags, dioramas and panoramas. The scale, colour and brashness of the posters had an enormous impact on the public but more especially on a nascent advertising industry which had so many of its clients among the Opera house, theatre and general entertainment fraternity. Barnum's ideas and methods quickly travelled to Europe by way of touring American circuses and minstrel groups.[23]

Tickets and Programmes in the Nineteenth Century. Until the early-nineteenth century, all tickets (save those for semi-private concerts) guaranteed admission only. Particular places could only be reserved if servants physically occupied seats in advance of their employer's arrival. The reserved seat did not become a regular feature of events until the 1830s when differential seating arrangements and associated pricing systems – lucrative for the promoter, and irresistible for class-conscious audiences – were introduced.[24]

Handel Festivals. A love of scale, patriotism, romanticism, novelty and spectacle certainly dominated the demeanour of the British and European musical scenes in the middle of the nineteenth century. This trend is perhaps best exemplified by the enormous Handel Memorial festivals which towered above the myriad events of regular public music-making. The first one took place at Crystal Palace in 1857 following on from the optimism generated by the Great Exhibition six years earlier.[25]

The Great Triennial Handel Festival held at the Crystal Palace in 1862 was accompanied by a programme printed by Robert K. Burt of London which throws a good deal of light on The Crystal Palace Company's arrangements for the spectacle and includes an account of the employment of colour and letter coding for the tickets. The event took place over three days and involved some four thousand performers. The programme carries this justification for the scale of the production:

2.4

> A festival in London in the present day must produce the broadest and grandest effects, to enable it successfully to compete with what may be termed "everyday occurrences".

Intricate or plain ticket designs reinforced the status of the seating. The more expensive ones offered a dose of Handelian bombast and over elaboration particularly in their passe-partout borders. Needless to say, all tickets for this series, low or high in price carried the all-important factual details of performance times, transport arrangements, access points and availability of printed music.

Programmes for concerts in nineteenth century London were either of the traditional letterpress kind, imparting a minimum of information or alternatively, elaborate lithographic confections, influenced by the greater visual conceits and informality of Parisian venues. These were intended to impart a similar air of abandoned reverie and animated social intercourse. A 1901 Royal Holborn Theatre of Varieties programme shows the large facade of the music hall above listings of available drinks and idealised Chéret-type women, accompanied on the reverse by the billing and an advertisement for music publishers, Francis, Day & Hunter. [26]

Designing the Modern Poster, c.1890–c.1955.

Modern advertising emerged from the mid-nineteenth century ferment of rapid technological advances and consequent mass-production of new consumables. The advertisers' mastery of scale as seen in the Barnum campaigns was enhanced by the employment of talented colour lithographers who, with their sophisticated understanding of autographic line, subtle tone and flat areas of colour, added a new dimension to the business of poster production. Conventional letterpress posters had been enlivened in the nineteenth century by developments in woodcutting and engraving. Even-so, variations on established eighteenth-century type-faces like the so-called fat-face, white-line, outline, reversed, shadowed or Egyptian, even when combined with woodcuts, coloured inks and a liberal deployment of exclamation marks, could not match the freedom and excitement of the lithographed sheet.

2.5.a

The modern poster first surfaced in the second-half of the nineteenth century in the wake of colour lithography advances in other commercial spheres. It was, from the beginning, dominated by images rather than words and stemmed from the hands of artist-designers rather than printers alone. Artistically-competent posters had already been seen in small-format adverts promoting new book titles for a growing readership in the 1820s and '30s while general chromatic and typographic freedom had been won to an extent on song-sheets of the 1840s. When poster formats began to increase so as to match the scale and impact of large American posters, the development of the modern European poster was inevitable.

Jules Chéret. One of the first artists to produce large, individualistic lithograph posters was Jules Chéret (1839–1932). His first colour poster was for the opera *Orphée aux enfers* by Jacques Offenbach (1819–80). Executed in 1858, it marked the turning point in music poster design. The calligraphic quality of his black and later blue figure outlines and novel *crachis* 'spatter' technique contrasted sharply with the colour-stencilled, relief-print posters of earlier decades. His images of animated, roseate young women (known as 'Chérettes') who were to be seen 'floating' in the poster's indeterminate picture space, owed not a little to the aerial conceits of the eighteenth century decorative rococo painter, G. B. Tiepolo (1696–1770) whom he so admired. His innovations were undoubtedly perfected in his café-concert posters to which he brought a healthy supply of new and exciting imagery redolent with convivial, risqué atmosphere.

2.12.a

Toulouse-Lautrec and other Poster Artists. Henri Gabriel Ibels (1867–1936), Georges de Feure (1868–1943) and Adrien Barrère (1877–1931) all produced elegant, colourful concert posters in the manner of Chéret for the concert venues of Montmartre in the 1890s as did Henri de Toulouse-Lautrec (1864–1901). [27] The latter's posters are unsentimental character portraits of performers he knew well, set in moody halls based on those he frequented in the Montmartre quarter of Paris. The hard-edged realism of these posters is even more pronounced in some of the gaunt concert portrait posters of Théophile Alexandre Steinlen (1859–1923), Leopold Stevens (1866–1935) and Lucien Metivet (b.1863 d. before 1930). They triumphed as poster artists at this bustling period, offering impressions of night-time venues populated by alluring though often world-weary performers.

2.5.b

As in the previous century, hall and theatre facades like that of the *Moulin de la Galette* were painted and decorated to advertise adjoining gardens, drink, and the all important *bal,* enlivened by more transient 'residency' posters. The attracting powers of such highly-decorated venues (both inside and out), heavy with painted scenery, ornamental fixtures, fittings, posters, and stage curtains posted with dozens of Chéret's sheets should not be underestimated.

British posters at this date did not exhibit the same florid, sensual qualities being directed more at the promotion of established, 'legitimate' theatrical entertainments and much influenced by the silhouettes of the Beggarstaffs (the poster designers James Pryde (1869–1941) and William Nicholson (1872–1949), working together: 1894–98). British design reserve is well-illustrated with a poster for the musical comedy *Little Miss Nobody* by Sir Bernard Partridge (1861–1945). The sheet displays a rather plain female figure who is safely ensconced within a conventional theatre-bill layout, complete with prosaic letterpress billings and production credits.[28]

Between the Wars. The successful and respected Dudley Hardy (1867–1922), inspired by Chéret's figures, devised the relatively lively 'Gaiety Girl' character for posters promoting the musical comedy *A Gaiety Girl,* first produced in 1893. Stylistically his designs owed little to Paris being more in keeping with the sober but *2.7.a* impressive economy of the Beggarstaffs.

As in France, poster designing in Britain gained in status, resulting increasingly in the hanging of the ephemeral, informative sheets on the walls of fashionable galleries. This trend had undoubtedly been set by the British poster exhibitions organised by Edward Bella in 1894 and 1896.[29]

From the 1880s to the 1930s, posters were mainly dominated by refined, 'flat', Beggarstaff-derived, 'early modern' *plakatstil* (poster style) imagery, evolving first of all in and around Berlin as simple visual messages for the speedy pace of modern life. These messages were mass-produced in their thousands, using fast and flexible offset lithography printing machines. The process had been developed initially in 1875 for tin printing but was also seen to work equally well for any weight or surface of paper, particularly that needed for exposed poster sites. There was still a call for locally-produced, poster paintings, which were essentially 'one-off' posters, but they at best lasted only a few weeks as their pigments were held in a medium more dilute than that used in the heavier, oil-based printing inks.

The secondary role of the poster as an expressive vehicle for fine-design continued into the twentieth century and indeed the poster became an experimental field for illustrators and designers wishing to translate some of the exciting formal revolutions of modernism into an acceptable,

decorative context. The expressive, personal abstractions of Cubism, Futurism, Suprematism and Constructivism did lead to the creation of poster styles more appropriate to music particularly evident in the designer of Paul Colin (b.1892) whose Léger-like tendencies (Ferdinand Léger 1881–1955), are thoughtfully tempered by the art deco practitioner's love of surface patterning. *2.13.a* This modification of the 'uncompromising' obscurantism of modern art, so often dismissed by a public wary of art divorced from everyday applications, played a critical part in exposing progressive imagery and typography to a mass-audience. This remains today in record sleeve design where the most rarified of abstractions are readily 'consumed' as enjoyable optical diversions.

Rock 'n' Roll 'n' Psychedelia.[30]

Early 'pop and roll' merchants chose to rely on cheap, easily-compiled posters for the promotion of the cavalcade, a 'showcase' package put together by the likes of promoter Alan Freed (1922–65). These posters were, at best, low-quality representations of young 'stars' or at worst, posters using the nineteenth-century device of visual variety through the use of differing type sizes relieved only with a generous sprinkling of star shapes amongst the names. The distribution of such 'boxing-style' sheets was confined to particular streets and was directed at a distinct audience.

In the 1950s, Hatch Show Print of Nashville frequently elected to print from relief-blocks of earlier decades, sometimes even using blocks of nineteenth-century origin. Block-cutter, Will Hatch, whose career in the poster business began in the 1920s, leaned heavily on traditional methods of direct-cutting and the expedient recycling of imagery to promote musical performers as they came and went in the '50s. Promoters like Colonel Tom Parker would insist on supervising Hatch's selection of imagery and type for posters of his protégé, Elvis Presley. British concern for 'pop-poster' aesthetics on the whole also left much to be desired. The momentum of a fickle, undiscerning teenage market, happy with the packaged tours arranged by Larry Parnes and others proved sufficiently strong to override worries about style and even moral niceties. The presence of pastiche Cliff Richard (b.1940) performers on stages across the country was to be expected but the appearance of posters carrying pictures of Cliff 'look-alikes' supported only by the line *'This artiste will appear here tonight'* was exploitative.[31] The use of stock promotional photographs or cheap cavalcade and 'boxing-style' sheets did not stop until the control of 'popular' music and its marketing was taken out of the hands of show business entrepreneurs by the musically and visually more advanced second generation of musicians and promoters. They turned quickly to Pop Art and Psychedelia for arcane graphic imagery and promotional tactics.[32]

The Psychedelic Poster. Psychedelic posters are characterised by formal distortions and jarring, 'mobile' colour combinations of one primary set-off against its complementary secondary (such as red against green). Ambitious colour experimentation ('day-glo' inks had already been introduced by Globe Printing in the 1950s), was combined in the screenprint stencil process with the frequent use of split ink-feeders to produce unique rainbow effects particularly successful when time was taken to heighten effects by overprinting. Central to the psychedelic poster's make-up were the 'customised', hand-drawn nature of the letters which looked back to highly-stylised examples seen in the work of art nouveau, art deco, jugenstil and Vienna secession artists. Several poster artists also received inspiration from the more legible though no less inventive nineteenth-century wooden letterpress faces. The art of William Blake (1757–1827), Alphonse Mucha (1860–1939) and Aubrey Beardsley (1872–98), (the latter receiving exposure in an exhibition at the V&A Museum in 1966), also had a marked impact upon the creative endeavours of psychedelic poster artists. Experimentation was not restricted to colours, lettering and iconography; conventional poster paper was set-aside by some designers who printed their posters on foils and plastics while others took to issuing circular posters or posters with edges dramatically scorched with blow-torches. Frequent inclusion of erotic forms and Eastern mystic symbolism completed what were, in retrospect, a richly-eclectic, but remarkably cohesive 'family' of sheets. These posters grew out of and flourished in the 1960s underground music scene pervaded by LSD, cannabis, pirate radio stations, clubs and permissiveness.

The psychedelic movement so far as it touched the music business, began with a single poster, the so-called 'seed', for the Charlatans'

appearance at the Red Dog Saloon, Virginia City, Nevada in 1965. It was partly designed by the band's leader, George Hunter, whose other single-colour poster designs on one-colour papers for bands like the Byrds, stood alongside the 'seed' as stylistic markers for those who followed him.

Other important and popular psychedelic poster artists who were part of the West Coast scene were Victor Moscoso (b.1936), and Stanley Mouse (b.1921?). They were part of the Family Dog co-operative which, together with Wes Wilson (b.1937), designed dozens of outstanding posters which helped to give a consistently exciting face to venues like the Fillmore, the Fillmore West and the Avalon Ballroom. The poster team *2.14.a,b* working for Bill Graham (b.1930), the promoter of these venues, was given sound economic advice and practical help from veteran printer, Levon Mosgofian, who had begun his career as a lithographic stone printer in the 1920s. He introduced them to an economical method of setting-out posters, tickets and postcards of the same coloured image on a single sheet so that it was required to pass only once through the press to produce all necessary publicity.

Wilson attributed the success of his graphic confections to a number of factors apart from the experiences afforded by LSD. To begin with he had trained as a conventional printer which gave him an insight into the possibilities and limitations of the trade. To this practical understanding was wedded his artistic appreciation of Jungendstil, Expressionism, and Vienna Secessionist typography.

The aesthetics and attitudes of the established fine-art and up-and-coming pop and op-art worlds slipped easily into the psychedelic psyche. It was therefore inevitable that posters and handbills rapidly became images to buy and collect as works of art divorced from any promotional function. Small runs of silk-screen posters for small-scale events were too limited in their number to satisfy a larger market hungry for the kaleidoscopic imagery. They were reproduced using high-speed, offset lithography and sold in stores all over the world, supplied by highly professional reproduction and distribution companies. One American poster store proprietor, Ben Friedman, enhanced his displays with elaborate lighting rigs modelled on the light shows of the day.[33]

In London, similar post-rock and roll collaborations between experimental musicians and young artists produced a healthy, college-based musical scene, supported by an English version of American psychedelia. The alternative magazine IT (*International Times*) offered several graphic designers the space to develop layout and general design skills. In early 1967, one of them, Michael English (b.1942), teamed-up with Nigel Waymouth to form the design group, Hapshash and the Coloured Coat, and produced concert posters, shop fronts and even record sleeve designs for their own records, inspired frequently by word of mouth reports of the new images and techniques *2.15.a,b,c* then surfacing on the American West Coast. Their distinctive exploration of the idiom proved to be exciting enough to catch the attention of Jimi Hendrix (1942–70), who commissioned a Hapshash poster for the promotion of one of his American concerts at the Fillmore Auditorium, (OA 103).

Late in 1966, IT launched a weekly nightclub called *UFO* founded on the multi-media attractions of psychedelic 'happenings' and employed Michael English to design the promotional posters. Aware, like many American entrepreneurs of the commercial potential inherent in long-term sales of desirable imagery, record producer Joe Boyd established Osiris Visions to print and distribute post-spectacle runs of posters. He was swiftly followed in the same business by a second firm, Big O Posters, partly owned by IT.

Osiris were involved in the design of colourful passe-partout framed posters into which changing concert-club details could be added for shows at the Saville Theatre Shaftesbury Avenue, promoted by the Beatles' manager Brian Epstein (1934–1967).

Epstein, rather like Bill Graham, was somewhat wary of the novel, psychedelic lettering appearing on his posters and complained as a concerned businessman about levels of legibility.

By the late 1960s, the 'exclusive', 'illegible' psychedelic stylings of the contemporary American and British music poster had become a familiar language of communication proved by the fact that in 1969, *Photolettering Inc.* issued a *Psychodelitype* catalogue of psychedelic type-faces to serve the hundreds of youth-oriented merchandisers keen to capitalise on the art-form's fashionable status. The hand-crafted, localised nature of the psychedelic poster was lost.[34]

Popular Spectacles of the 1970s and 1980s.

The Beatles went their separate ways in 1970. Just six years later, the Sex Pistols went into the the studio to record what was to be their first single, *Anarchy in the UK*. In the short space of time between these two significant events, British contemporary music underwent some startling transformations. The graphics these developments spawned are many and varied but can be broadly categorised as three distinct streams flowing out of the record industry, then and now, the most powerful and influential part of the music business. The first of these streams carried accomplished rock acts like the Moody Blues, Led Zeppelin, The Rolling Stones, and Pink Floyd who engendered polished, lavishly packaged LPs , only performing live at a relatively small number of large and prestigious venues across the world. live LPs were issued to placate those unable to witness the shows in person. Their concert posters were not unrelated to those of psychedelic America in terms of their colour and optimism, but even so, many suffered from promoters' and designers' possibly unconscious striving to reproduce on paper, the finish and monumentality of the groups' recorded music by the use of air-brush and modified photo-imagery.

The second stream is that made up of 'pop' stars operating mainly as 'glam-rock', 'teeny-bopper' and disco acts releasing singles over a short period which were promoted through magazines, radio and television. Their performances were, almost without exception, ones which were confined to recording or television studios. When live performances were given, they were promoted by small advertisements in the music and general press, announcements in fan club magazines and by the general hype in the rest of the media, fascinated by the adolescent hysteria surrounding them.

The third stream of the record industry at this date was made-up of acts operating sometimes in, sometimes beyond the narrower courses of the other two. David Bowie (b. 1947), Elton John (b. 1947) and Roxy Music, working in this stream all wrote and recorded artful music in the studio, but they also mounted theatrical stage shows and happily posed for any magazine photographer wanting to portray them as teenage idols.

In short, live spectacles for musicians, were, more than ever, brief but intense moments in which they, as 'distant' recording-stars performed for their record-buying fans. Time, money and creative talent was channelled less into the slow build-up of a career through regular live work and more into producing new singles and LPs, publicity shots, 'stagey' live shows, merchandise and the occasional musical feature film.

In the middle of the decade, teenagers in Britain who felt socially and musically disenfranchised joined forces with fresh musical talent, new entrepreneurs and new designers, possessing a desire to challenge the bland, all-pervasiveness of 'glam-rock', 'teeny-bopper' pop, disco and progressive rock. As in mid-1960s Britain and America, a new music, new audience and independent promotional vehicle was again emerging, this time to create an irreverent, punk and new wave movement, active as often on stage as in the studio.

Malcolm McLaren (b.1946) promoted live appearances of the Sex Pistols using dada-like performance modes of the late 1960s situationists. Helped by artist Jamie Reid (b.1947), who designed a memorable and significant series of flyers, posters and record sleeves involving degraded photo-images, 'undisguised' layout techniques, and 'cheap', 'blackmail lettering' torn from newspapers.[35]

The aggression of the Sex Pistols' music, allied to Reid's revolutionary graphics, had a tremendous impact on the direction of live music promotion in the late 1970s. It showed young musicians, young entrepreneurs and a new generation of graphic artists that controversial behaviour, fanzines, and 'covert' promotion of hastily organised or 'secret gigs' all underpinned and promoted with 'low quality' graphics were together, the perfect confection with which to compete with or even by-pass ossified establishment channels *2.16.b* and methods.[36]

Punk and new wave concerts could be 'exclusive' events that proved to be endurance tests for many young people unable to identify with some of the more extreme elements of the idiom. What was offered for the majority was a cleaned-up, commercialised New Wave, sold and promoted in conventional ways, heard on radio, seen at medium sized city venues and college campuses.[37]

Festivals. The huge outdoor Pop festivals like Monterrey (June 1967), and Woodstock (August 1969), developed their own promotional momentum generated within the alternative culture of psychedelia and therefore had little need for conventional graphic devices particularly at a time when the notion of selling was so abhorrent to many. Attempts to promote and control Woodstock through conventional graphic means were thwarted by a site change, vast number of visitors and general unpredictability of the venture; poster details and ticket reprints for the new venue became redundant as the entire Woodstock spectacle turned into an unregulated free festival. In the 1960s and '70s, popular music festivals in Britain had a reputation for offering good music in poor, ill-managed sites. They have continued to take place in the '80s, and have been joined by a large number of longer, multi-media arts festivals and jazz festivals across the country offering a wider choice of music, together with better standards of presentation, accommodation and sustenance. Many popular annual festivals need a minimum amount of graphic support, maintaining a positive profile in the minds of festival audiences that can last all year. Dates, billings and ticketing details do, however, change, and must of course be circulated in print. This information is supplied in the pages of the music press and on a small number of street posters in large cities. Jazz festivals, too, have a core of devotees who only need to receive low-key prompts about imminent events in jazz magazines and on radio. The rise however, in the number of jazz festivals, large and small, during the '80s has encouraged the appearance of high-profile posters designed by establishment artists like Eduardo Paolozzi (b.1924) of which a design of his for the Soho Jazz Festival is an example. More determined marketing ploys have also emerged in the general press and in specialist record shops. Both new and long-established music-oriented city festivals are advertised in the general press sometimes supported by small but clear graphic 'icons' that symbolise the essence of the spectacle. These black and white symbols are usually reductions of larger colour illustrations printed on leaflets and distributed across the country to be picked-up in concert-hall foyers, tourist information centres and public houses.[38]

The spectacular 'mega' rock conscience-cum-charity concerts staged at Wembley over the last few years in aid of famine relief or universal suffrage in South Africa have their roots in the Rock Against Racism and Red Wedge concerts of the late 1970s and early '80s. The tremendous amount of electronic media coverage afforded these powerful shows has pushed the role of posted or hand distributed promotional paper and graphics somewhat into the wings.[39]

'Serious' Spectacles, 1950–90

Since the end of World War II, a sizeable proportion of orchestral and operatic music, old and new, has been supported by overtly modern graphics.

Müller-Brockmann. This tendency is exemplified in the 1950s and '60s by the work of Josef Müller-Brockmann (b. 1914). His unemotional De Stijl and Jan Tschichold (1902–74) inspired work is a precise, restrained typographical application of principles that result in marvellously controlled posters belonging to the so-called Swiss School of
2.13.b design. Of special note is his 1950s and '60s work for the Tonhalle-Gesellschaft in Zürich, in particular its *Musica Viva* series promoting with discreet layouts of small, sans-serif lowercase lettering, the neo-classicism of Hindemith and the atonality of the 'Second Viennese School' of Arnold Schoenberg (1874–1951), Alban Berg (1885–1935) and Anton von Webern (1883–1945). In spite of growing popular familiarity with modern poster forms, such typographical asceticism would have been viewed as inappropriate for the promotion of more energetic popular musical forms.

Anxious to dress their promotional material in a style which would appeal to young audiences bombarded by 'fashionable' contemporary design, promoters of 'serious' music in the 1980s more than ever employed 'modern' designs for
2.19 their posters and programmes.[40]

Bob Linney, The Arts Council and the 'Bloody Loud LCO'. Of particular note are the imaginative and impressive series of Arts Council Contemporary Music Network posters and flyers designed
2.17 by Bob Linney (b.1947), throughout the '80s. These 'uncomplicated' sheets are the result of several distinct stages of production. Initial *Rotring* pen 'roughs' on plain paper are submitted for approval before the colouring can begin. Gently-blended hues are introduced into an enlargement of the chosen drawing by way of a silk-screen process involving repeated manual application of selected semi-opaque inks through a limited number of stencils. From a group of these uniquely coloured prints, just one is chosen as the 'camera-ready' art-work. When the image is prepared for

offset litho printing, the 'solidity' of colour is maintained by the omission of the lined-screen which, if used would break-up the image into tiny regular dots.

Contemporary, 'rock'-inspired promotions of 'serious' sounds have recently gone a stage further with The London Chamber Orchestra, some of whose promotional copy for 1990 read: *'Boring and tedious classical presentation gone forever.'*

An even more outspoken statement headed their June 1990 London concert poster. It read: *'Classical Music Bloody Loud'.* This street poster, dominated by a 'luminous' giant strawberry, was used to promote their 'Power Concert' at The Hammersmith Odeon. This rock-like spectacle 2.18 used a PA system of thirty thousand watts, enhanced by lighting, a stage-set and back projection film all linked-up to a computer. According to an LCO press advertisement in *The London Evening Standard* of 8th June: Mozart and others would now be *'As loud as Def Leppard or Simple Minds'.*

Let's Dance.

In popular music, dancing is the fundamental connection between the pleasures of sound and their social realisation in the libidinal movement of bodies, styles and sensual forms...the moment where romanticism brushes against reality. *Chambers, I. (1988) p. 135.*

In the early-eighteenth century, the ball existed outside any commercial framework. It was still a semi-private, well regulated event of significance which facilitated social intercourse. There was, however, even at that date a place for graphics to adorn the dance-fans, ball-cards and dance tutor-books of 'ball-culture'. Later in the century, balls more frequently followed a public concert attended by paying participants made aware of their occurrence by the distribution of letterpress handbills.   2.1

By the nineteenth century, informal dances and formal balls in both town and country had become many and varied, serving the needs of local inhabitants attending social events on a regular basis. As the century drew to a close, the less decorous dances, particularly those offering eating and drinking facilities began to be promoted not only through handwritten signs and by word-of-mouth but by the lithographic poster.

World War I entertainments for troops and civilians alike often focused somewhat naturally on the dance, so that when, after the war, radios, gramophones, jazz bands and dance orchestras were 'broadcasting' dance tunes, ballrooms and restaurants did their best to offer space for all those who were keen to maintain the habit of gliding across the dance floor.

Dancing remained popular in the 1930s, receiving much encouragement from the many big-bands of the Swing Era. As before, locally displayed, hand-painted posters and a few printed sheets by local artists were the most effective form of advertising in conjunction with the dance-hall's own sign-board. World War II again stimulated demand for dances which has continued unabated to the present. In the 1960s, American psychedelic poster artists designed sheets to express the multi-sensory, experimental dances and in the '70s, thousands of semi-professional DJs and club owners commissioned small runs of printed flyers, tickets, business cards and some hand-drawn sheets to promote the discos held in every city, town and village across the world.

House Style. A dedicated graphic style grew out of a dance-orientated youth culture in the late 1980s. The movement was centred on the acid-house phenomenon in Britain and Europe which had its origins in the underground dance sounds of Black Chicago's 'house' music. It first became apparent in Britain in 1985 with all-night acid house 'raves' which were in essence large, near-spontaneous dances to be experienced in Home Counties barns 'just off' the M25 and equally well in Mediterranean resorts catering for the young, North-West European holiday maker. Musically, acid-house was marked by a fast and compulsive dance beat, a high incidence of digital samples from other records and sampled screams, all peppered with the abstract timbres of analogue synthesisers. [41] The 'raves' were characterised by the large number of dancers and their endurance levels, a feature too of 1970s and '80s 'all-dayers', soul weekends and the marathon dances of the first-half of the century.[42]

Acid-house imagery, like its music, has appropriated elements from many sources including day-glo colours, '60s 'smiley' faces, CND peace symbols, flowers and the graffiti 'match-stick men' of New York artist Keith Haring (1958–1990). All of these elements were fused together to symbolise the presence of non-stop, euphoric good times. People were eager to adopt and spread this visual message and so, not surprisingly, bought the printed t-shirts, sweat-shirts, baseball caps, jewellery, record sleeves, and magazine covers that sported it.

Flyers, however, were at the root of acid-house image generation and distribution. A distinctive and preferably fresh flyer design was needed for each new 'rave'. Pirate radio stations could broadcast venue details but flyers were, in the end, the best way of communicating most cheaply and effectively the necessary details and excitement of a 'rave'. Many dance organisers invented and drew their own flyer designs with the result that they display a calligraphic, often humorous, home-grown style, photocopied or printed at local high-street print shops.[43] Other equally popular, club-based musics like rap, hip-hop, latin, funk and rare groove have their own symbolism and fashions which receive inspiration from grafitti, home computer graphics or from some of the longer-established musical iconography of American popular music.[44]

2.20

Popular Musical Theatre.

In the Middle Ages, miracle players walked temporary stages and enlivened their stories with song. In the sixteenth and seventeenth centuries, courtly musical spectacles and the development of opera maintained and enlivened the drama and music tradition. By the eighteenth century, Italian opera was well-entrenched across most of Europe, appealing to all tastes, but it usually had to compete with lighter, though still refined combinations of drama and music.[45] In the nineteenth century, 'serious' instrumental and operatic music-making and mass-entertainment shows continued to prosper as did those 'lighter' forms of drama and music typified in Britain by the operettas of Gilbert and Sullivan. Working together between 1871–96, they produced several popular and influential comic operas which helped to strengthen the habit of regularly going to see and hear musical theatre productions. Edwardian musical comedy, epitomised by *The Arcadians* and *The Merry Widow* became common features of London's West End theatres. The structure and content of these shows was partly based on American comedy dramas and burlesques of the 1880s and '90s, which presented fanciful tales in contemporary settings.

2.6

American musicals of Broadway and Hollywood in the first half of the twentieth century had roots in American performances of European operas, popular French musical theatre, and a vibrant indigenous musical culture of Minstrelsy, Burlesque and Vaudeville.

In Britain, a stage-orientated musical show business rooted in both these American musical dramas and in the British music hall reliance on 'turns', determined the direction of much home grown 1950s and early '60s 'pop' music. it was 'show-cased' in touring packages, and was helped in no small measure by the new medium of television which demanded 'traditional', stage-like spectacles.

West End Sights. In the late 1960s and early '70s, the stage musical scene in Britain was given a tremendous lift by 'rock operas' like *Hair, Jesus Christ Superstar* and *Godspell.* This particularly lively and successful British brand of the genre has, in the 1980s come to dominate theatres all over the world in the guise of musicals like *Cats,* 1.21.a *Miss Saigon* and *Les Misérables.* These shows have been promoted, packaged and 'branded' as internationally relevant packages signalled by the powerful show 'trade marks' designed by Dewynters and Russ Eaglin. Beginning his career by designing a Palladium poster for Judy Garland (b.1922), Eaglin is now a creative director at Dewynters the theatrical printers, based in London's Leicester Square. Their simple but effective show logos are not just the preserve of theatre hoardings, handbills, posters (many of which are displayed in a century-long tradition across the surfaces of London's buses), programmes, song-books and record sleeves but additionally range across countless t-shirts, mugs and towels.[46] Such is the demand for tickets for these shows, that handwritten notices in the windows of theatre ticket agencies like Keith Prowse (established by Keith and Prowse in 1815) and First-Call are sufficient to 'sell' them and any other stage spectacle that has a acquired a good reputation.

Bill Posters.

'Fly-posting will always happen. It caters for the impromptu stuff. There'll always be the last minute gig.'
Dave Walker quoted in *ES, The Evening Standard Magazine.* February 1990. pp. 42-6.

The business of promoting a concert is only complete when the printed sheets are pasted-up on a wall. The people who do this are known as bill posters who have a long and sometimes controversial history of their own.

A plethora of bill posters on the crowded streets of eighteenth century Paris resulted, in 1722, in the city authorities taking steps to control activities by limiting pasting activities to a body of forty, uniformed and literate people.

The experiences, sites and problems of the bill poster operating in the wide open spaces of America in the late nineteenth and early twentieth centuries were of a very different nature. The logistical problems of effectively posting diverse sites across states were occasionally overcome by dedicated, well-organised teams of repute headed by the likes of Mrs. H. E. Root of Wyoming and Mrs Chas Ducket of Illinois, whose posting route encompassed forty one towns.[47]

In the late 1970s and '80s, London's illegal bill or 'fly' posters pasted adverts for 'serious' and 'popular' concerts on to vacant shop fronts, corrugated sheeting at derelict sites and on traffic light control boxes, supplementing promotional material seen in the press and at venues. Prime sites at road junctions, along main routes into central London and at other prominent spots were (and still are) 'regulated' by particular bill posting outfits. For example, Terry 'the Pill' Slater who began his trade in the early 1970s and had, in 1988 with his fellow operator Dave Walker, eight vehicles and twenty two staff. Each team of fly posters toured the streets with small batches of sheets so as to avoid possible mass-confiscation of a consignment if stopped by the police. Even so, it is estimated that some three hundred smoothly stuck sheets (cockled sheets tear easily), could be put up in a day.[48]

Notes

1 For a theoretical account of the rise of concert as commodity, supported by useful historical data see Attali, J. (1985) pp. 46–51 & pp. 57–62.

2 In terms of the number of individual messages they convey, they recall the theatre bills of the nineteenth century and the 'cavalcade' posters of the 1950s.

3 Posters promoting spectacles have, since the advent of sound recording, often also embodied graphics and copy which promote associated record releases thereby directing the viewer towards the record shop as well as the concert hall. For an account of live performance itself as promotion see Frith, S. (1978) pp. 93–4.

4 See Walker, J. A. (1987) pp. 60–4 on posters in the home and on the street.

5   See Blumenthal, A. R. (1980). There is a *descrizioni* by Michelangelo Buonarroti the Younger for the wedding feast of Maria de Medici 1600, complete with libretto of songs performed.

6   In the 1680s, York House on the Strand was built complete with a public music room at the request of a group of musicians. The noted Hanover Square Rooms opened in the eighteenth century. Less exclusive and costly concerts arose about these venues in the taverns, generating their own dedicated promotional material.

7   Court music, street and church music continued to thrive but did so beyond the new field of commercial music-making. Midway between these polarities was to be found the professional concert performed at a stately house before an invited but paying audience. On the rise of commercial concerts in England, see Raynor, H. (1980) pp. 92–4. See also Tilmouth, M. (1983).

8   Leppert, R. (1988) p. 205.

9   At this date, instrumental performances in London were delivered by the Academy of Antient Music (sic), founded in 1728, 'Professional Concerts' beginning in the 1780s, and the Salomon subscription concerts which played host to Haydn in the 1790s.

10 In France, public concerts were predominantly bourgeois in conception fed by such organisations as the Concert Spirituel founded in 1725 which eventually grew into a significant musical vehicle for a number of European composers.

11 Details taken from a press advertisement featured in The British Library's *Haydn and England* Exhibition, 1989.

12 On the interesting relationships between public and private spaces for music and for an examination of Hogarth's engraving see Leppert, R. (1988) pp. 201–14. The Harry R. Beard Theatre Collection in the V&A's Theatre Museum has a Theatre Royal poster of 1746 for Gay's opera which lists date (but not time) of performance and the names of artists. Also listed are dancers and a notice about the addition of a pantomime. Ticket prices were thus: boxes: 5s, pit: 3s, First gallery: 2s, upper gallery: 1s. A notice about the need to refuse persons backstage access because of the need to effect smooth scene shifts is included.

13 See Tuer, A. W. (1881) pp. 48 & 62.

14 V&A Museum, 28689.J. One of the most comprehensive collections of tickets assembled at the time is that of Sarah Sophie Banks (1744–1818) which is now in the British Museum, supporting the view that systematic ticket collection was not unknown at this date.

15 See Paulson, R. (1989) cat. no. 110.

16 V&A Museum, 24475.7.

17 Both were exhibited at The British Library *Handel and England* Exhibition, 1989.

18 Much of this nineteenth century background material is based on the following works: Bailey, P. (ed.) (1986); Bratton, J. S. (ed.) (1986); Pearsall, R. (1973) & (1975); Russell, D. (1987); Weber, W. (1975) and Cooper, J. (1983).

19 As earlier with Haydn, composers like Weber and Felix Mendelssohn (1809–47) were invited as 'star' performers to conduct their latest works at special performances. Choral societies flourished as did brass bands and provincial orchestras like the Hallé, founded in Manchester in 1857 by Sir Charles Hallé (1819–95). In 1895 Sir Henry Wood (1869–1944) founded the Queens Hall Promenande Concerts which were taken up by the BBC in the 1920s.

20 Russell, D. (1987) p. 94.

21 A popular form of entertainment to be found in France at the same time were the café-concerts, cabarets and music halls. See Brody, E. (1988). These were paralleled in America by vaudeville and burlesque shows.

22 There was a continued interest in European composers (witnessed at least at the start of the century with the foundation in Boston of a Handel and Haydn Society in 1815). A lot of music was however fed by many European folk and Afro-American styles so that following black emancipation, indigenous ragtime and jazz would have the greatest appeal for the majority in America. Europe heard the developing musical styles of America as early as the 1820s, performed by black minstrels crossing the Atlantic.

23 Hendon, D. W. and Muhs, W. F. (1986).

24 See Weber, W. (1975) pp. 25–9.

25 It was undoubtedly modelled to an extent on the recruitment of 1,200 musicians by Hector Berlioz (1803–1869) for a concert at the 1844 exhibition of industrial products in Paris. Tickets for the first Handel Commemoration Concerts and for rehearsals in 1784 were sold from special offices opened in St. Albans Street and from music shops such as those of Longman & Broderip.

26 Enthoven Collection, V&A's Theatre Museum.

27 Toulouse-Lautrec also turned his hand to the drawing of song-sheets for the music and words of Richepin and Dihau, so immersed was he in the French musical scene.

28 Partidge's work was also considered suitable for another section of the music business as his '*original picture*' entitled *Inspiration* was used to embellish a record bag. (V&A Museum, E. 1785–1990).

29 By 1912, critical appreciation, both popular and establishment and the common participation of serious artists in poster generation led writers and designers to define the ingredients of a successful image from a psychological and aesthetic standpoint. See Price, C. M. (1922) pp. 1–14 and Kauffer, E. M. (1924).

30 Much of the material here is based upon Grushkin's encyclopaedic work: *The Art of Rock. Posters from Presley to Punk*, Grushkin, P. D. (1987).

31 Rogan, J. (1989) p. 77.

32 On 'first' and 'second' generation 'pop' and 'rock' management see generally Rogan, J. (1989) and Wale, M. (1972).

33 On light shows and music see Walker, J. A. (1987) pp. 101–5. Not to be forgotten in this context is Bonnie Maclean's ephemeral chalk-art which listed bands on the foyer boards of America's psychedelic music venues.

34 For a discussion of 'exclusivity' in a product see Sinclair, J. (1987) p. 57 and Tomlinson, A (1990) p. 27.

35 See Reid, J. and Savage, J. (1987).

36 Low-profile performance promotion is to be seen on a Pop Will Eat Itself picture disc, *Very Metal Noise Pollution*, 1989 designed by The Designers Republic which carries details of exclusive gig details for the fans: *'25/08 Powerhouse'* (V&A Museum, E. 728, 729 –1990.)

37 A majority of record-related tour itineraries of rock groups are advertised (often with record-release details) in the national press, in listing magazines as well as in the 'tour news' sections, 'gig-guides' and separate full-page spreads of the music press. On rock concert ticket promotion in general and for a discussion of the trend for profit-making residencies at large venues in Britain see White, J. (1990). An interesting development in joint concert and record promotion has been that of David Bowie and EMI in 1990, encouraging fans to phone a special phone-line and nominate songs to be performed on stage.

38 *The British Music Year Book* for 1990 lists two hundred and twenty Festivals in Great Britain of which 30 are jazz and 55 are folk. BMYB (1990).

39 See O'Hagan, S. (1990). Some cynics have linked the phenomenal success of new talent to world coverage of their appearances at these events.

40 There has also inevitably been a fair amount of traditionalism in poster and programme design because certain opera houses and concert halls believe their reputations and performances are expressed most effectively through conventional type-faces, 'classical' iconography, single colours and symmetrical layouts.

41 See Redhead, S. (1990) pp. 1–6.

42 The availability of a drug at 'raves' known as Ecstacy, which speeds-up heart rates attracted widespread media attention turning the phenomenon, its associated imagery and merchandise into fashionable commodities for many.

43 Most flyers are given-out on the street, picked-up in record shops or distributed at large gatherings like the *Freedom to Party* rally held in Trafalgar Square in 1990.

44 The selection in these genres of a particular visual motif is largely a matter for the groups and record labels who are anxious to communicate with a chosen sector of a segmented consumer market.

45 In Restoration France for instance, Rossini (1792–1868) invigorated a long-present trend for light opera in France which had grown with the Opéra Comique, founded way back in the late seventeenth century as a response to touring Italian troupes.

46 See Morley, S. (1989).

47 *Billboard* 7th December 1901, reproduced Cisda, J. and Bundy J. (1978) p. 109.

48 See Malone, P. (1990) and McAfee, A. (1988). The problem of illegal fly posting in Britain was raised in a 1989 waste paper debate in Parliament.

Selling the Musical Spectacle

Posters, Handbills and Tickets

Plates

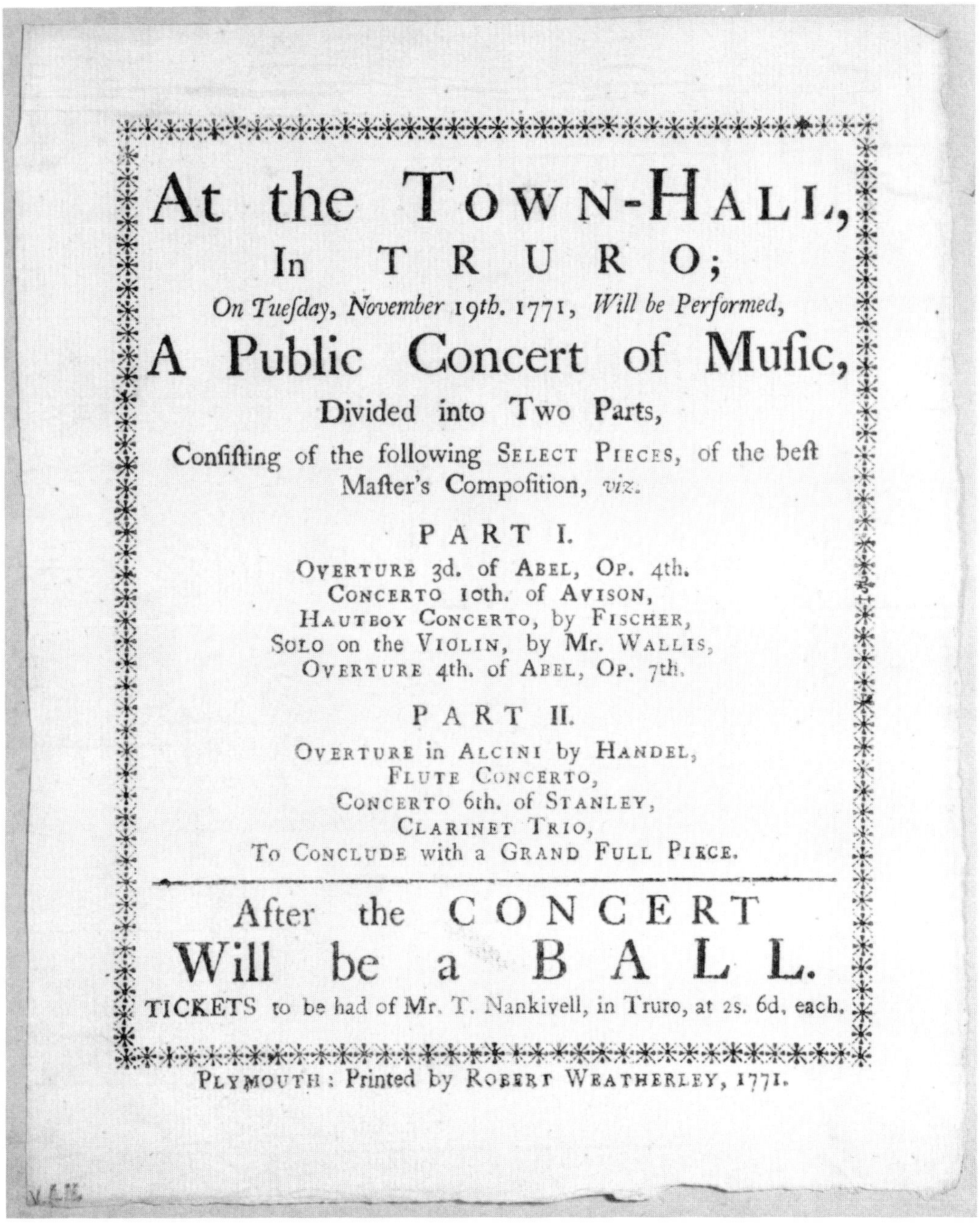

At the Town-Hall,
In TRURO;
On Tueſday, November 19th. 1771, Will be Performed,
A Public Concert of Muſic,
Divided into Two Parts,
Conſiſting of the following Select Pieces, of the beſt
Maſter's Compoſition, *viz.*

PART I.
Overture 3d. of Abel, Op. 4th.
Concerto 10th. of Avison,
Hautboy Concerto, by Fischer,
Solo on the Violin, by Mr. Wallis,
Overture 4th. of Abel, Op. 7th.

PART II.
Overture in Alcini by Handel,
Flute Concerto,
Concerto 6th. of Stanley,
Clarinet Trio,
To Conclude with a Grand Full Piece.

After the CONCERT
Will be a BALL.
TICKETS to be had of Mr. T. Nankivell, in Truro, at 2s. 6d. each.

Plymouth: Printed by Robert Weatherley, 1771.

PLATE 2.1 : Handbill. *Concert, Truro Town Hall.* Des: anon. Letterpress. Pr: Robert Weatherley. 1771. 19.1 x 15.9. E. 1130–1945. This modest but effective bill carries all essential information, lists the musical programme for the evening and lays emphasis on the ball which was to follow.

E 1228-1948

PLATE 2.2.a : Subscription ticket design

Handel Commemoration Concert, Westminster Abbey.

Signed R.S. ie: Robert Smirke (1753–1845). Line and Wash. 1784. Cut to: 14.0 x 13.8.

E. 1228–1948. Probably a preparatory drawing for 21030.5. shown below.

SUBSCRIBERS TICKET, West-Door.

2.2.b : Subscriber's ticket Handel Commemoration Concert, *Messiah*, May 29th, 1784. West-door. Des: Smirke. Ex: F. Haward R.A. Etching and stipple engraving. 21030.5. This ticket relates to the above design in respect of the principal figure at the tomb but there are many differences, most notably the adoption here of a portrait format. (See Handel/NPG (1985). cat. no.

PLATE 2.3 : Eighteenth century admission tickets.

Vauxhall Jubilee. 2d Door. Des: anon. endorsed in ink: '*Jona: Tyers.*' Etching. 1786. 28.1 x 21.7. E.183–1944.

The New Musical Fund. Des: J. Ibbetson. Ex: J. Thornthwaite. Etching. Late-eighteenth century. 23.0 x 15.0. 21030.11.

Mrs Stewart's Concert, Hanover Square. Des. & ex: I. Neagle. Etching. Late-eighteenth century. 12.2 x 17.4. 24473.5

Norwich Grand Music Festival. Ex: Delogati, Winchester Street. Etching and engraving.
    Late-eighteenth century 9.8 x 13.1. 29039 B.

For the Benefit of Mr. Salomon. Des: B. Rebecca. Ex: F. Bartolozzi. Etching and stipple engraving 1794.
    Plate-mark: 6.8 x 9.5. 21030.12.

Opera subscription ticket King's Theatre. Des: anon. Etching. Late-eighteenth century. 6.1 x 8.2. 24475.9.

Unused oratorio ticket, Theatre Royal Haymarket. Des: Bartolozzi(?). Etching and stipple.
    Last quarter of the eighteenth century. Plate-mark: 12.2 x 15.6. 24475.7.

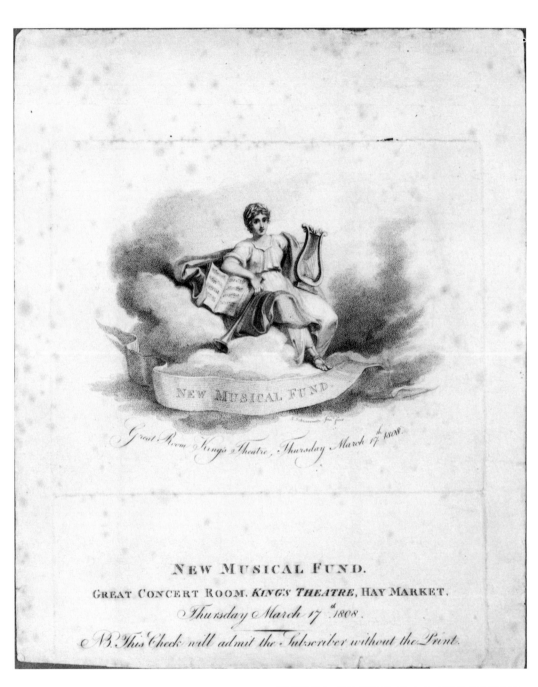

PLATE 2.4 : Nineteenth-century admission tickets.
The New Musical Fund. Great Room King's Theatre. Ex: N. Schiavonetti Junior (1771–1813).
Stipple engraving. 1808. 23.2 x 19.2. 28689.J. *Crystal Palace Grand Handel Festival, 1857.*
One guinea tickets *Messiah/Judas Maccabaeus/Israel in Egypt.* Des: M. Digby Wyatt. Colour lithography and letterpress.
Each c.10.6 x 17.9. 21032.12 to 21032.17. *Crystal Palace Grand Handel Festival, 1857. Judas Maccabaeus,* half-Guinea ticket.
Des: anon. Letterpress 8.9 x 12.5. 21032.28. *Birmingham Musical Festival. Messiah, Creation* and *Selection.*
Des: anon. Etching and stipple engraving. c.1823. 7.5 x 11.1. 28689.D, 28689 A. *Crystal Palace Triennial Handel Festival, 1862.*

Selection. Two-guinea ticket. Des: anon. Lithography and letterpress. 10.6 x 13.9. 24476.7. The general-purpose Passe-partout frames of Wyatt carry musical personifications, instrumental trophies and a portrait of Handel.
On the reverse is printed: 'price exclusive of railway fare. Correct editions of the book of words and of the music as performed are to be obtained in the Palace only on the day of performance.' The reverse of the 1862 ticket states that ticket holders who register their names will receive directions, police regulations in respect of carriages and particulars of the issue of the official book of words.

PLATE 2.5.a : Theatre-bill *Dibdin's Morsels of Mirth*
at the Mermaid Tavern, Hackney. Des: anon. Letterpress.
Pr: S. G. Fairbrother, Exeter Court, The Strand. c.1822–31.
47.8 x 22.8. E. 4776–1923. A large amount of information
about Dibdin's popular musical entertainment
is here made legible and attractive for readers
through the use of a varied selection of type sizes and faces.

PLATE 2.5.b : Poster. *Eugénie Buffet.*
Des. & ex: Leopold Stevens (b.1866). Colour lithography.
Late-nineteenth century. 121.9 x 74.3. E. 2419–1938.
Eugénie Buffet was a celebrated singer of a 'social realist'
school of performers. Here she is depicted as a ballad-
monger with her back to the viewer, performing a
song to her 'true' audience: the people of the streets.

PLATE 2.6 : Four colour lithography advertisement cards For Gilbert and Sullivan operatic
p roductions at the Savoy Theatre. Average size: 12.8 x 17.0. E. 1714 to 1717–1925.
These are chiefly all-purpose promotional adverts for the Savoy Theatre which are overlaid
with letterpress details of performances together with adverts for Liberty fabrics and the like.
E.1716–1925 lists the cast and states that *'on this occasion the opera will be conducted by the composer.'*

HMS Pinafore. Des: anon. c.1887.

The Mikado. Des: anon. c.1885.

HMS Pinafore. Des: anon. c.1887.

The Gondoliers. Des: Hildesheimer & Faulkner with A.
Havers. England. Printed in Germany. c.1885.

PLATE 2.7.a : Poster. *The Grand Duke* comic opera by
Gilbert and Sullivan at the Savoy Theatre. First produced 1896.
Des: Dudley Hardy (1867–1922). Colour lithography.
Pr: Waterlow & Sons Ltd., London. 76.5 x 49.6. E.1407–1963.
Here there are no fussy ornamentations or over-long lists of
secondary information. It is an economical street poster
designed to be understood at a glance.
Its effectiveness centres on its visual 'hook':
an isolated, black silhouette set against
a rich yellow background.

PLATE 2.7.b : Poster. *Greenwich Village*. Des: anon. Offset lithography.
56.0 x 71.0. E.2909–1980. Films offer pre-recorded music, promoted as 'star-studded' spectacles for a paying public.
Hollywood's use of 'stars' on promotional graphics looks back to the pre-film days of lyric and score promotion.
Its mastery of such promotional 'star' imagery ran parallel with, and into formulae being perfected by music publishers
and the burgeoning record industry. *Greenwich Village* is, perhaps ironically,the story of a serious composer
persuaded to stage one of his works as live Broadway review.

PLATE 2.8.a : Poster. *The Supremes.* Lincoln Center. Philharmonic Hall. 1965. Des: Joseph Eula. Offset lithography. Pub: Darien House Inc. NYC (re-issue). c.1973. 97.3 x 63.5. E. 323–1973. The actual profile of the Supremes, already a familiar sight on television and in magazines, is here formalised into a near-abstract, silhouette symbol. Note that the poster informs the viewer of the availability of tickets through mail order as well as the box office.

PLATE 2.8.b : Three concert programmes.

Royal Festival Hall, Paolo Silveri song recital, 1951. Des: anon. Line-block and letterpress. Pr: London Counties Press. 21.6 x 14.0. E.1336–1990. Inside are adverts for Silveri on Columbia and for forthcoming RFH events.

BBC Symphony Orchestra 1959-60 Season at the Royal Festival Hall. Des: Laurence Bradbury. Offset lithography. Pub: BBC. Pr: Baines & Scarsbrook Ltd., London and Uxbridge. 22.1 x 15.7. E.1335–1990. Inside are programme notes, a photograph of conductor Sir Malcolm Sargeant (1895–1967) together with adverts for The Decca group, Scotch magnetic tape, Steinway pianos, and Grundig (Great Britain Ltd).

BBC Symphony Orchestra 1963-4 Season at the Royal Festival Hall. Signed Biro. Line-block. Pr: King & Hutchings Ltd., London and Uxbridge. 20.8 x 13.2. E.1337–1990. This design is a loose adaption of Henrion's RFH symbol. inside are adverts for *EMItape,* the conductor Colin Davis on HMV, BBC broadcasts, Fergusson stereograms and Challen pianos. The lyre and crown symbol designed in 1950 by F.H.K. Henrion (1914–1990) for the London County Council RFH, was deployed on cutlery, staff uniforms, the hall's fixtures and fittings

PLATE 2.9.a : Concert programme.
Jazz at the Philharmonic (JATP).
Illus: David Stone Martin, programme des: Jack
Higgins. Offset lithography Pr: Compton Printing
Works. 1962. 26.8 x 20.9. E.1330–1990. Jazz
promoter Norman Granz (b. 1918), employed the
talents of Chicago illustrator David Stone Martin to
add distinction and character to some two hundred
record sleeves in ten years. Martin's vibrant,
blotted-line portraits of jazz people were
stylistically akin to those of the influential Ben Shahn
(1898–1969) and the approach of both is reflected in
Andy Warhol's sleeves for Kenny Burrell (b.1931)
on Blue Note, and for Count Baise (1904–1984)
on RCA Victor. The Granz JATP live showcase
(first heard in 1944), has on this 1962 British tour
bill, Coleman Hawkins (1904–1969) and
Ella Fitzgerald (b. 1918) amongst others.

PLATE 2.9.b : Poster. *American Folk Blues*
Festival,
Frankfurt, 1968. Des: Gunther Kieser (b.1930)
Offset lithography. Pub: Darien House Inc.,
NYC (re-issue). 113.3 x 84 3. E.398–1973.
A real guitar provides the setting for Kieser's
graphic evocation of Black America's history
and music. To be seen are pictures of
Abraham Lincoln, Martin Luther King,
a banjo-playing minstrel,

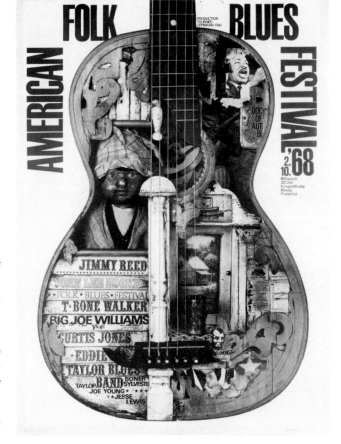

PLATE 2.10.a : Poster. *Montreux Jazz Festival, 1971.*
Des: Bruno Gaeng. Offset lithography.
Pr: Corbaz S.A., Montreux. 69.8 x 37.2. E. 1319–1974.
Here Gaeng's matter-of-fact treatment of the poster's text
recalls the typographical clarity of designs by Swiss compatriot
Müller-Brockmann. To evoke the music of the festival an
illustration of schematised musicians, instruments and
sound waves have been set into the ultimate musical device:
a creature which is half-bird, half-brass horn.

PLATE 2.10.b : Music press advertisement *Regular*
Music in Scotland. Compiled by Barry Wright. Appearing in
the *New Musical Express* October 14th, 1989, p. 48. 42.5 x
30.0. Private collection. A compilation of 26 Scottish
concerts from October to December are arranged inside
the large, lower-case 'r'. Compressing so many group names
and logos on a single page often vividly illustrates the relative
strength and originality of a particular design. Note the
guitarist in The Cult's concert advert who has been taken
from their *Sonic Temple* LP sleeve.

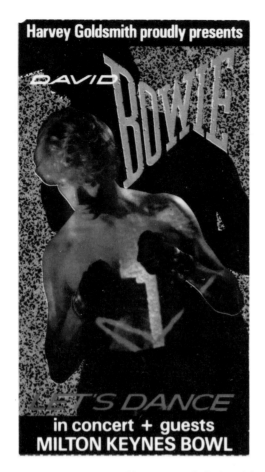

PLATE 2.11.a : Admission tickets The Milton Keynes Bowl leg of the David Bowie *Let's Dance* tour promoted by Mr. Harvey Goldsmith. The design is based on the Mick Haggerty, Greg Gorman and Derek Boshier sleeve work for the *Let's Dance* LP, 1983. Offset lithography. 11.2 x 6.5. E. 1631, 1632–1990. The back of the tickets carry information on the filming and sound recording rights of the promoters, a warning against the use of cameras and tape recorders by the audience, a notice reading: *'Beware of pirate programme sellers!'*, travel details and promotional copy for the availability of the *Let's Dance* LP and Cassette at HMV shops.

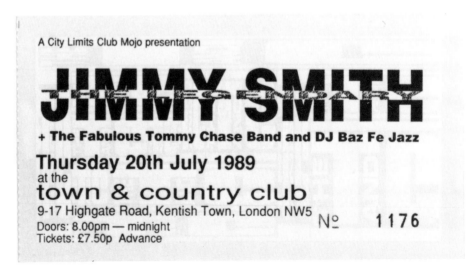

2.11.b : Admission ticket Jimmy Smith (b.1925) at The Town and Country Club. Des: Falconer Press. Offset lithography.1990 Pr: Falconer Press St. Albans. 6.6 x 12.4. E.1354–1990. This was designed for the Town and Country Club on an Apple Macintosh computer using the Aldus *PageMaker* software programme.

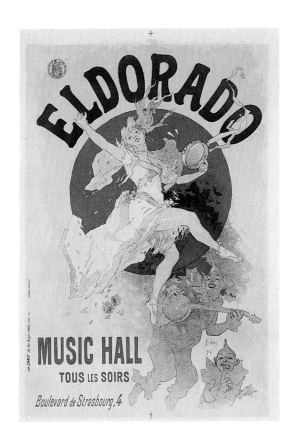

PLATE 2.12.a : Poster. *Eldorado Music Hall.*
Des: Jules Chéret (1836–1932).Colour lithography.
Pr: Chaix, Paris. c. 1894. 59.2 x 40.4. Circ. 163–1913.
A musical, limelight world of escapism peopled by
dancing girls and clowns is created here through
Chéret's careful tonal modelling, transitory poses
and indeterminate spatial placements.

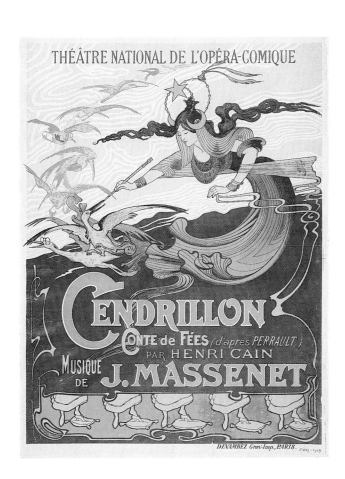

2.12.b: Poster. *Cendrillon.*
Theatre National de L'Opéra-Comique.
Des: anon. Colour lithography. Pr: Devambez,
Paris. 1899. 79.2 x 59.8. E. 527–1939.
The opera, (Produced Paris 25th May 1899),
was adapted by H. Cain from a story by Perrault.
Here, an outstanding art nouveau design has
had its figurative elements transformed on
the sheet into a single organic pattern.

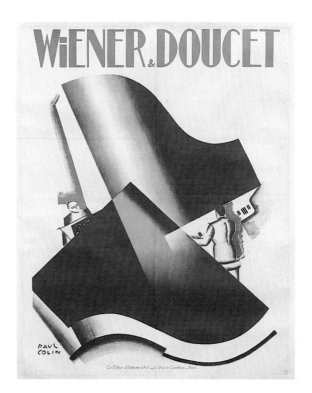

PLATE 2.13.a : Poster. *Wiener and Doucet*.
(A Piano duo) Des: Paul Colin (b. 1892).
Colour Lithography. 1925. 159.4 x 119.4. E. 506–1929.
The influence of Casimir Malevich (1878–1935) and
Ferdinand Léger (1881–1955), is perhaps detectable
in this design's stylisation of the two pianos.

2.13.b : Poster. *Juni–Festwochen*
Zürich Stadttheater. Des: Josef Müller-
Brockmann (b. 1914). offset lithography.
1950. 127.5 x 91.5. E. 929–1965.
An early example of Müller-Brockmann's
posters for 'serious' concerts in Zürich.
Müller-Brockmann and his Bauhaus-
trained colleague Max Bill were
instrumental in devising the Swiss School's
typographical principles. Letters had to
be subordinate to words, words had to be
subordinate to sentences which, in turn,
had to be subordinate to the main
message and overall design.

PLATE 2.14.a : Poster. *Moby Grape Dance Concert.*
Des: Victor Moscoso (b.1936). Offset lithography.
Pub: Family Dog Productions. 1967. 51.0 x 35.5. E.733–1970.
The two figures in this design are taken from a oil painting
by Jean Auguste Dominique Ingres (1780–1867) entitled
Thetis Imploring Jupiter, (1811). At the lower edge of the
sheet, some 13 ticket outlets are listed in an ordinary,
more legible type-face.

2.14.b : Poster. *Chambers Brothers and Iron
Butterfly at the Avalon Ballroom.* Des: anon.
Offset lithography. Pub: Family Dog Productions.
1967. c.51.4 x 35.5. E.731–1970. Here, the designer has
modelled his main lettering on jungendstil typeface
known as *sezession* which was first used in about 1902.

PLATE 2.15.a : Poster. *The Move at The Marquee.* OA 109.
Des: Hapshash and the Coloured Coat. Michael English (b. 1942)
and Nigel Waymouth. Screenprint. Pub: Osiris Visions. 1967.
75.2 x 49.5. E.36–1968. The 'OA' number refers to the issue
sequence of poster firm Osiris Visions Ltd.
The name Hapshash is a corruption of Hatchepset,
an Egyptian queen of the 18th Dynasty.

2.15.b : Poster. *UFO Coming* OA 104. Hapshash and the
Coloured Coat. Screenprint. Pub: Osiris Visions Ltd.,1967.
74.3 x 50.0. E.28–1968. The UFO posters were printed in
limited numbers and fly-posted at select sites.

2.15.c : Poster. *Pink Floyd. CIA UFO.* OA 114.
Hapshash and the Coloured Coat. Screenprint.
Pub: Osiris Agency Ltd. 1967. 73.3 x 55.0. E.22–1968.

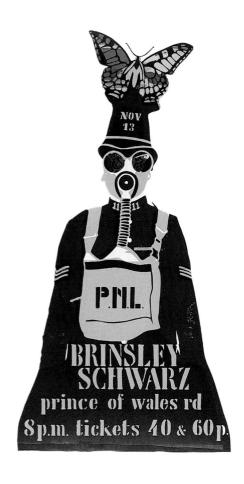

PLATE 2.16.a : Poster. *Polytechnic of North London. Brinsley Schwartz. November 13th, 1974.* Des: Martin Walker (b. 1947) and Bernadette Brittain (b. 1953) of The Red Dragon Print Collective. Screenprint. 76.2 x 51.1. E.409–1975. The confrontational aspect of this poster in some ways recalls the assertive, autonomous images designed and printed by students during the Paris riots of May 1968.

2.16.b. : Fly poster (proof?). *Buzzcocks at The Vault,* Presbyterian Church. North Road (Brighton). Des: anon. Screenprint and felt marker pen on classifieds section of *The Brighton Evening Argus.* 1977. 41.9 x 31.4. E. 3019–1990.
Not having the talents of The Buzzcocks' Manchester designer Malcolm Garrett to hand in Brighton, local promoters and designers produced this 'rough and ready' poster which is as much a statement about the New Wave belief in independence and immediacy as it is a promotional device.

PLATE 2.17 : Eight Handbills

Arts Council–Contemporary Music Network in
Association with The South Bank Board.
Des: Bob Linney. (b.1947) 1987–1989.
Average size: 21.0 x 14.8. E. 1357 to 1360–1990,
E. 1362 to 1365-1990. Linney is now applying the
same 'intuitive' approach to the design of
record sleeves for UB 40 and The Beloved.

PLATE 2.18 : Poster. *Classical Music Bloody Loud.* London Chamber Orchestra. Des: Carroll, Dempsey & Thirkell. Offset lithography. 1990. 150. x 101.2. E. 3026–1990. This poster advertises the amplified LCO concert which was to be *'As loud as Def Leppard or Simple Minds.'*

PLATE 2.19 : Concert handbills and programmes. Various sizes (the largest: 41.9 x 29.7).

Komische Oper Berlin at the Royal Opera House. Des; Dominic Carroll. 1989. The image of Offenbach as Bluebeard by Dietrich Kaufmann. E.1367–1990.

London Sinfonietta. Queen Elizabeth Hall. South Bank Centre. 1987–88. Des: anon. E. 1366–1990.

Steve Reich and Musicians. Des: anon. South Bank Centre. 1988. E. 1368–1990.

LSO at the Barbican. Des: Assorted Images. Pr: First Impression. 1988. E. 1369–1990.

London Philharmonic International Series. Des: anon. Royal Festival Hall. South Bank Centre. 1989–90. E.1370–1990.

Eighth Almeida International Festival of Contemporary Music. Des: Paton-Walker Associates. Pr: Pinpoint Offset. 1988.
   E.1371–1990. The design reflected the world premiere of Michael Finnissy's opera, *The Undivine Comedy* and used
   images of sculptor Kate Blacker's stage-set.

London Sinfonietta. South Bank Centre Resident. 22nd Season. 1989–90. Des: Peter Clare. Typeset by Solo Graphics.
   E.1372–1990. Vital, clean-cut graphics are designed to attract the eyes of potential concert-goers as they pass
   through venue foyers.

PLATE 2.20 : Dance and music club flyers. Various techniques. Various sizes (largest: c.21.0 x 14.9).

Chumbaloo. York Place, Leeds. Des: anon. 1990. E.1338–1990.

Surrealism at Limelight, London. Des: anon. 1988. E. 1339–1990.

Mayhem, Kilburn Park. Des: anon. Euphoria & Keyman Promotions. 1990. E. 1340–1990.

Dance Party 90 at the Arena. Des: John Clynch. Inhouse Promotions. London N8. 1990. E. 1341–1990.

The Catfish Club, Brighton. Des: anon. c.1989. E.1342–1990.

Spizzvision at the Marquee Club, London. Des: anon. 1989. E.1343–1990.

Musika. Shaftesbury Avenue, London. Des: anon. 1989. E. 1344–1990.

No Turning Back. Queen's Club, Colnbrook. Des: anon. 1990. E.1345–1990.

Superstition at Gossips, London. Des: anon. Organised by Julia Franks, Nick Turner and Robert Sabel. 1990. E.1346–1990.

Paradise at Gossips, London. Des: anon. 1990. E. 1347–1990.

Musika Mix't Shaftesbury Avenue, London. Des: Akeem Eze. 1990. E.1348–1990.

Synergy, London. 1990. E.1349–1990. *More Kaos.* Des: anon. c.1989. E. 1350–1990.

B 52s at the Town And Country Club and record release flyer. Des: anon. 1989. E. 1351–1990.

Sin at the Astoria, London. Des: anon. c. 1989. E.1352–1990.

A small selection of flyers showing the huge variety of imagery stemming from dance and club organisers seeking to create a lasting impression on the streets of London in the late 1980s.

SELLING PACKAGED SOUND
WAX CYLINDERS TO CD.

'You're a cube (a square from squaredom, that is) if you don't dig the doings in disc-and-dungaree circles. Fact is, the cats are real gone about platters merchandised by original photographic design. A newly issued album is the summit (that's higher than the tops, brother) when the hi-fi combination of printing and paper gives with visual rhythms.'

Copy encircling 'Rock Roll', an experimental, double-page spread from
Westvaco Corporation's journal *Westvaco Inspirations* 210 1958.
Designed by Bradbury Thompson.
Reproduced in *Graphic Design in America. A Visual Language History.*
Walker Art Center. Miniapolis Catalogue. NY 1989. p. 110.

SELLING PACKAGED SOUND
WAX CYLINDERS TO C.D.s

Sound Packages:
Their Function and Form.

In the first half-century of their existence, sound recordings supported the two established fields of commercial activity. When played, they encouraged song-sheet sales, boosted the renown of artists and indeed, for a time, were thought by some to have a place on the concert platform as mechanical performers. In the late-twentieth century, changes in this commercial symbiosis have occurred as records have come to dominate the music business. The uneasy relationship however, between performer and pirate as first seen in the eighteenth century continues.

> An hour after the Godfathers finished their Reading Festival set, pirate tapes of the performance were on sale in pre-printed sleeves.
> *The Observer*, Section 5, p.3. September, 1988

These Reading pirates were not like their predecessors, selling poorly-printed song-sheets of popular tunes but rather pirated sound recordings (bootlegs), of public performances. The late-twentieth century Godfathers fan at the festival (and elsewhere) would have been looking to repeat the live musical performance by buying a recording (legitimate or otherwise) of the band's Reading appearance. Here, and in every case of packaged sound-selling, the presence of the recording is signalled by the ubiquitous devices of paper and ink.

As is the case with song-sheets, the graphics which service packaged sound seek to differentiate the commodity from its neighbour and communicate its aesthetic character and specific content. As before, their sophistication is determined by all concerned: composers, performers, 'publishers' (or record companies) bootleggers (!) and the consumer. Legitimate recordings are additionally supported by promotional graphics seen on hoardings and in the press.

Attali has observed that with sound recording, music:

> 'becomes a material object of exchange and profit, without having to go through the long and complex detour of the score and performance anymore.'[1]

The 'nickle-odeon's' metal disc, the phonograph's wax cylinder, the gramophone player's shellac and vinyl records, and the tape machine's plastic cassette and tape were, and still are ideal musical commodities. In one sense they are already music made flesh; these encoded metals and plastics can be handled. The temporal immaterial aesthetic of the music is tamed and fixed.

The Nineteenth Century Background. The last quarter of the nineteenth century, saw a demand for more live music and new compositions but more importantly for 'on-tap' music for the home and communal environments wherein the markets were increasingly musically-passive. These demands were met and given further momentum by the rapid advances in audio-technology being made in America and Europe.[2]

Sales of musical box cylinders and discs, were heavily reliant on inventive advertising copy and rich imagery in the press which was at one remove from the cumbersome, ultimately mundane boxes and disc machines themselves. Inside the lids of many of these mechanical music-makers were delicate colour lithograph scenes of playful children. Other lids sported more ornamental, monochromatic passe-partout cartouches framing hand-written song-titles. 'Nickel odeon' discs themselves carried lithographed title information and occasionally some figurative imagery. They were packaged in large paper and card albums, and in many ways foreshadowed the book-like record albums common in the 1930s.

Twentieth Century Revolutions.

Phonograph Cylinders. The shiny, often coloured surface of the wax cylinder generated not mechanical music, but for the first time a facsimile of a human voice or musical instrument and were at the same time, smaller, and generally more 'user-friendly' than musical box cylinders and 'nickel-odeon' discs. Initially they were only available to the public via coin-in-the-slot machines, but finally became available for domestic use in the 1890s. Each delicate wax cylinder was carefully housed in a lambs-wool lined cylindrical cardboard box topped by a neatly fitting lid, creating for the first time, an intimate relationship between the com-

3.1 modity and its packaging. There was tremendous variety in the quality of the colour lithography bands of paper wrapped around these boxes. All promoted the record company and its associated hardware, and in the case of Edison releases, additionally carried 'signed' facsimile framed photographs of the phonograph's inventor Thomas Alva Edison (1847–1931), thus personalising these otherwise 'disembodied', mass-produced articles. Song-titles and names of artists had not yet seeped into the package's imagery but was instead to be found embossed in the cylinder's upper rim in white lettering and on a plain circular paper label pasted onto the box's lid. The more artistically adventurous companies decorated their new product by applying formulaic, diminutive art nouveau tendrils, frames and idealised feminine forms to their cylinder boxes. Such motifs were indebted to the standard press and poster imagery of turn-of-the-century Europe and America. The range of regular lithographic inks used for these images was carefully enhanced by the inclusion of 'gold' highlighting, no doubt in part intended to match the bright and brassy components of the phonograph.

In contrast to the fragile and difficult to mass-produce wax cylinder of the phonograph, the more durable, easy-to-store flat gramophone disc, devised by Emile Berliner (1851–1926), could be made in great numbers using moulds taken from etched zinc masters. From 1893 (just two years after the issue of the first phonograph cylinder catalogue by the Columbia Phonograph Company), Berliner's discs were being played on gramophones driven by electric motors. This breakthrough quickly paved the way for serious commercial exploration of the new format which had, until this date chiefly been regarded and promoted not as a serious musical device but as a toy. As with the cylinder, popular dance material proved to be technically and commercially more suited to the new medium, and was recorded in abundance in the late 1890s. The advent of the ten-inch disc in 1901 and the double-sided disc in 1903 marked the beginning of the end for the wax cylinder.

The Gramophone Record Bag. The outstanding musical mimicry of the phonograph and gramo-

phone initially had sufficient charisma to attract and develop a paying audience without a great deal of reference to the recording artists themselves. When pictures and names of performers were used, they tended to be there as endorsers of the record-playing hardware and record companies as much as to promote their own record releases. *3.5.b* Colourful, high-quality portraits of 'stars' and extensive 'liner notes' that offered the consumer enthusiastic accounts of the sound within, together with biographies, musical analysis and instrumentation data did not become a standard feature of the packaging until the late 1940s when microgroove 'Long Playing' (LP) albums and singles appeared in the shops.[3]

Established performers took readily to packaged sound. In 1898, the music-hall artiste George Lashwood laid down his voice on disc and in the following year the contralto Dame Clara Butt (1872–1963), who frequently sang royalty ballads to promote song-sheets, cut a disc with Kennerley Rumford. Although Dame Clara Butt's name and reputation as an interpreter of particular songs continued to have a place as promotional devices on the front of song-sheets like *Down Here* published by Enoch & Sons in 1915, in the following year, not only her name but her face could be seen gracing the colour lithography posters of London's underground railway, there to promote her recordings for Columbia. *3.17.a*

Plain paper or card 'bags' protected and packaged these early shellac records. Circles were stamped-out of the middle of the bags so as to expose the recording particulars printed on attractive circular labels at the centre of the discs. These variously designed and coloured labels were dominated by a record company's logotype or emblem, placing little graphic emphasis on the featured recording artist. The most famous example is the HMV (His Master's Voice) label, showing a dog (Nipper), seated beside a gramophone player. It was based on a painting by Francis Barraud (1856–1924) which he sold to The Gramophone Company, who first used it on their record catalogue of 1900.

Exceptionally 'stars' were given a high-profile billing of sorts which relied on simple colour coding. The mauve labels used from 1904 on the one guinea releases of Dame Nellie Melba (1861–1931), regally flagged her vocal presence to all familiar with the code. The exclusivity and higher price of these releases was undoubtedly just a marketing device exploiting consumer snobbery, a device which is still in play in the 1990s.

The Late Twenties, Thirties and Forties. Record bags made out of a wide range of coloured or plain card and paper continued to carry a variety of graphic imagery and typography. Large companies issued generic 'house' bags printed with their logotypes and paired-up with the now common accounts of the unbeatable sound quality and tech-*3.4.a* nical wonders of their related players and radios.

Competition from high-quality radio sound in the 1920s combined with an increased interest in live dance bands and the 'talkies' called for a bold response from the record companies wanting to avoid the fate of music publishing. The introduction from 1925 of electrically recorded discs and amplification served as the basis for the response that came. Decca bravely embarked on a bold, price-cutting campaign which proved to be the salvation of themselves and much of the industry. The availability of inexpensive records combined with favourable hire-purchase agreements on players and the rise in the number of provincial retailers further boosted interest in records. In 1931, The Gramophone Co. and The Columbia Gramophone Co. merged to create Electrical and Musical Industries (EMI); an all-powerful operation capable of surviving market fluctuations and strengthening the industry with its regular introduction of new talent and technical improvements.

Survival of the industry was certainly helped too by the emergence of the Juke-box in the late 1920s and '30s and the manufactured excitement of heavily-promoted hit parades. record bags at this time continued to lay great emphasis on the quality of packaged sound as for example in the 'scientific' presentation of acoustical data on a bag for the Brunswick Electrical Light Ray Process and the Holloway Stores retailer bag which claimed gramophones and records to be *'Better Than an 3.4.a,b Orchestra'.*

3.5.a In the 1940s, Hollywood dominated the popular end of the musical spectrum epitomised by its movie musicals and Tin Pan Alley take-overs. Hollywood studios, not content with their share of the music business cake moved-in on radio stations in a bid to extract further profits by raising air-play fees. Radio, initially a competitor of the record business, came unwittingly to its aid. Instead of relying on Hollywood for new material, radio stations instead looked to small record companies to provide them with the then up and coming grass

roots music of black and white America. This gradually led to wider exposure of young talent in the 1950s which was seized upon by other independent recording studios experimenting with the new technology of magnetic tape.

The trying social circumstances of World War II stimulated musical consumption, lifted record sales and paraded a vast amount of new American taste and talent to the European market. Record sales rose further after the war when microgroove LPs, singles and then stereo recordings became widely accessible to everyone.

Microgrooves paper and ink. In 1949, Columbia introduced the microgroove vinylite 33 and a third rpm LP and Victor issued the seven inch, 45 rpm 'single'. Microgroove records with their delicate surfaces, and troublesome static called for the development of a different kind of package. A smooth, usually plain paper bag protecting the record surface was introduced to cover the record and slide with it into the more robust, all-enveloping outer sleeve. Devoid of the shellac bag's cut-away centre which had exposed label details, the un-cut, laminated fronts of the vinylite sleeve were used to give a higher graphic profile to the record's title, composer and performer. This information was often set in letterpress, and printed into an offset lithography passe-partout frame, embellished with familiar company logotypes. These front covers were backed by a so-called paper 'slick' which gave companies plenty of space to print all kinds of subsidiary copy. *3.6.b*

Soon sleeves personalised with photo-portraits of a smiling Elvis Presley, Frank Sinatra or 'serious' performer began to appear. Unique to a particular release, they were especially attractive to the teenage market which was starting to reject their diet of generic sleeves served-up by the formal counter service system of traditional outlets. They now favoured 'one-off' sleeve designs on sale in those stores adopting the self-service, 'browserie' approach.

Record sleeves were no longer insignificant, interchangeable bags of protection, used only to promote peripheral products and services. They were now carefully designed and printed signal and index devices of dedicated imagery and texts. At home, sleeves were increasingly being read and studied like books, sometimes for up to forty minutes as the record played. In the 1960s, more and more record companies, designers and musicians saw the LP sleeve's communication potential

and devised gatefold formats, fold-out sleeves and
lyric sheets turning it into a fetishized commodity
3.10 in its own right.

Although many seven and ten inch releases
followed the LP sleeve formula some were still
akin to the paper bag of the shellac 78 rpm,
retaining a label hole surrounded by logotypes.
They were enlivened with abstract 'modernistic'
3.7 designs or single-colour illustrations of teenagers
3.8 listening to records at home or at a party.

Corporate Designs.

Giving commodities a readily recognisable, 'family' character over and above the unique 'star'
imagery of a particular release can give a company
an advantage over its competitors. By repeatedly
using the same trademarks, logotypes, colours and
layout, an 'unchanging', all-pervasive corporate
image is planted into the consumer's subcon-
scious, cultivating a 'brand loyalty' of sorts.

The graphic creation of a company character
had already begun in the late-nineteenth century
with phonograph and gramophone manufacturers. This trend was well established in the 1930s,
being epitomised by the strong visual identities of
HMV and Decca, and from the 50s to the present
by companies big and small like Deutsche Grammophon, Blue Note, ECM (Edition Contemporary
Music), Land, Fon Records, and 4AD.

In the 1960s it was recognised that perhaps the
ultimate means of addressing discrete bodies of
consumers lay not with the production of a cohesive label image but in the creation of a 'corporate' graphic identity for a single group. This is
exactly what the design team Hipgnosis achieved
for Pink Floyd and what Roger Dean achieved for
Yes in the 1970s. With their finely airbrushed fantasy scapes and hyper-real surrealities, Hipgnosis
and Dean developed a strong, readily identifiable,
visage for their clients, ironically at a point when
many composers, performers and consumers
were choosing to describe their music as 'pro-
3.23.a gressive rock'. In the 1980s and '90s the corporate
identity strategy is alive and well in the hands of
illustrators like Derek Riggs who has created and
upheld an unmistakable figure of science fiction
fantasy for the sleeves of heavy metal group Iron
Maiden. David Smart and Accident have provided
a strong identity for Holly Johnson's solo releases,
inspired by the vorticism of Wyndham Lewis
(1882–1957).

Where There's Art on the Sleeve.

In the 1950s and early '60s, freelance sleeve and
poster designers, photographers and illustrators
were far less common and had a much lower profile than they do today. Many of the larger record
companies relied almost exclusively on graphics
produced by their in-house design teams populated by the likes of Maurice Roach (b.1912). Roach
joined Decca in 1939 and soon went on to become
their Advertising Manager. He helped to plan their
promotional leaflets and poster artwork, often
executing many of the drawings himself. By the
1950s, Decca was calling on the services of a large,
in-house art studio, and smaller art department for
press advertisements, its own photo unit, sleeve
note drafting section and a separate promotional
office. Supplementary photographic material, particularly that used for 'serious' releases came to
Decca as colour transparencies from commercial
picture libraries and the archives of bodies like the
National Trust.[4] The rather inflexible 'production-
line' nature of sleeve design at Decca may have had
some bearing on the company veto of several
'individualistic' designs submitted by The Rolling
Stones for their LPs in the 1960s which have still
not seen the light of day.

The Beatles. The Beatles were the first group
of composer-performers to achieve sustained
universal appeal and influence. Their music,
imagery and marketing was a heady mix of American rhythm 'n' blues, imaginative studio production, youthful bravura, art school libertarianism,
big-business acumen and talent. Their recordings
sold in millions, while their humour and photogenic faces sold millions of newspapers, magazines and films worldwide. Their approach to self-
promotion and record packaging demonstrated
the means by which other young groups might
seek graphic enhancement from their peers
rather than from design teams of another generation working in corporate isolation.

In the 1960s, groups like The Who, The Grateful Dead and The Moody Blues chose to see the LP
record sleeve as a visual extension of the aesthetic
and philosophical statements within. No longer
conceived simply to attract the new listener but
the knowing devotee, obscurantist music and *3.9*
images emerged and matured together, largely *3.19*
inspired by sub-cultural movements and pop-art
painters.[5]

In the pre-punk seventies, established marketing ploys in the rock LP field were joined by a renewed pop assault on the younger consumer, which relied relying on disco, radio, television and press exposure to sell songs issued as 45 rpm singles packaged in identical 'house ' bags or as LPs fronted by unimaginative group poses.

The Sex Pistols. Punk and New Wave grew from the live club performances of young British musicians who rejected disco dancing, vacuous pop and arcane rock. The raucous immediacy of the music was different but hardly novel. Their contentious attitudes, fashions, lyrics and graphics too, were in marked contrast to the prevailing trends but were not entirely spontaneous creations of a disaffected underclass. The nihilism and aggression of American bands like The Velvet Underground and later The New York Dolls (working for a time with Malcolm McLaren) and even the more caustic aspects of British heavy metal groups laid important foundations for the calculated unpredictability of punk's shock tactics epitomised in McLaren's and Reid's creations: The
3.21 Sex Pistols. Art school portrayal of a musical
3.22 movement had been important in the 1960s and was now important once again. Art school-trained designers were called upon to devise a cohesive graphic focus for the diffuse noise and bluster that constituted Punk and New Wave. Again, music became a rallying point and vehicle for art school experimentation. Commenting on the Manchester scene in the late 1970s, graphic designer Malcolm Garrett (b.1956), pointed-out that many creative people were nurtured by the punk movement in the North West, including himself, the rock journalist Paul Morley, (who later gave form and direction to the Frankie Goes to Hollywood phenomenon), graphic designers Peter Saville (1955) and Mark Farrow, Tony Wilson founder of Factory Records, and Kevin Cummins, photographer. Garrett maintains that punk:

> wasn't dole queue rock it was an art school [movement which]...opened the doors for a lot of like-minded, like-driven individuals operating in different spheres, the Sex Pistols said "its not about the music", but that brought everyone together.
> Malcolm Garrett in an interview with the author, 1989.

What groups like the The Sex Pistols, The Buzzcocks, The Damned and The Clash and graphic designers like Jamie Reid (and to a lesser extent) Malcolm Garrett accomplished in the creative flux

that was Punk and New Wave was the *apparent* rejection of the accepted notions of finish, refinement, training and technique .

The significance of this was that it spurred hundreds of genuinely untutored young musicians and designers across the country to exploit a 'DIY' *3.13* approach to self-expression and advancement. Economic factors and aesthetic 'preferences' for degraded black and white imagery and second-hand lettering militated against the appearance of slick colourful albums or glossy magazines. Graphic expression via black and white photographs, newspaper lettering, scissors, felt markers, paste, and tape surfaced in fanzines and spilled-out into record shops to supplant the plain, seven inch sleeves of the early 1970s. Gaining experience and winning reputations in the relatively free artistic environment afforded by Punk of the late 1970s, many British graphic designers went on to work in the mainstream music and non-music areas of the following decade.[6]

Post-Punk Orientations.

For a short time in 1976 it *was* about music. The photogenic faces of pop were briefly eclipsed by 'un-designed', monochromatic artwork drawn at home and reproduced in high street print shops. By the early 1980s, a radical reversal took place. The Sex Pistols had split-up, The Jam, Elvis Costello (b.1955) Ian Dury (b.1942) and The Pretenders were producing new wave songs with mainstream appeal. Contracts with large record companies were signed. The radical edge of punk and new wave graphics had entered the mass market resulting from the inevitable fusion of Punk's 'DIY' attitudes and big business manufacturing. The consumer-generated sounds of punk and new wave had been anathema to manufacturers wanting to address mass-markets. It had to be schematised, diluted and mass-produced. 'Alternative' punk culture quickly became an off-the-peg style.

At the same time, a vibrant, apolitical fashion-oriented new romantic club scene arose. It owed not a little to the 1970s pop-disco axis, but was, none the less firmly rooted in Punk's reliance on consumer-led stylings.[7] Support for the movement came from magazines like *Smash Hits* edited by Nick Logan, formerly of the all black and white *New Musical Express*. He saw the potential for a colourful magazine as a vehicle for the sartorial displays of good-looking, *Top of the Pops* performers. At the same time, magazines like the *Face, i-D* and *Blitz* discussed all that was to be seen on 'the street', bought in shops and heard in the clubs. These publication added buoyancy and drive to the post-punk music business vessel in the same way that *Sky Magazine* and *Q Magazine* do at present. These last two titles are specifically targetted at those who consume music through screen and CD machines at home. As Readhead has observed:

> To enthuse about the 'product' to be consumed - whether it is football, music, clothes or what ever, however critically, implies some kind of support for the industry that produces the commodities for our multiple pleasures.[8]

Assorted Images and Malcolm Garrett. Duran Duran and Culture Club, products of the post-punk realignment, sought to work within the musical establishment but retain control over career development and presentation. To do this, they elicited strong graphic interpretations from Garrett, Kasper de Graaf and their design group, Assorted Images.

Studying typography, graphic communication and psychology at Reading University before returning to his native North West to study graphics at Manchester Polytechnic, Garrett was well prepared to apply principles of layout, inspired by a knowledge of Dada and Constructivism. On entering The New Oxford Street Virgin record shop in 1977 to buy a Sex Pistols' single, Garrett witnessed the uncompromising music and *image* of the Sex Pistols on a video screen. He rapidly became enthused by the punk movement in general and began designing for the Manchester punk/new wave group The Buzzcocks, all the time working in close liaison with the musicians and their manager Richard Boon. Boon founded the New Hormones label and presided over the first independent production and distribution of a punk/new wave recording, namely *Spiral Scratch* by the Buzzcocks.

This particular coterie held well-formed views on music as a 'product' and saw the need to protect the evolution of a band's corporate image from record company design teams who might dilute the subtleties of any emergent group persona. television and radio may sell one record, but a group's career had to be constructed from a variety of well-controlled, visually-centred initiatives.

In the early 1970s, Barney Bubbles (1942-1983), had generated, in the spirit of the 1960s

community crafts tradition, an entire image for the live appearances and sleeve art work of rock band Hawkwind, fashioned entirely from within the confines of the immediate group. Garrett fully acknowledges the significance of this approach for much of his own work. For Garrett, like Bubbles, the sleeve was only a part of the story,

> the other part was how the band looked on stage, how they presented themselves there, how their merchandising was sold, how the records were advertised, how the street posters were done, how the sheet music was sold, everything.
>
> Malcolm Garrett in an interview with the author, 1989.

The use of the record's catalogue number for the Buzzcocks' LP *UAG 30159* on the throw-away outer bag was intended to make clear some of the sophisticated commercial mechanics at work on Assorted Images sleeves. In the 1980s, Garrett and Assorted Images continued to pursue what the music business terms the 'total concept', employing more, carefully devised generic and 'associated images' for groups like Simple Minds.

In the 1980s, Garrett's and Assorted Image's work for Duran Duran, Culture Club and Simple Minds has always respected the integrity and career plans, personalities and musical statements of the clients, i.e. the musicians and managers, providing a sleek, modernistic but ultimately conventional visual encasement of the 'stars' as and when required.

3.24

In the same 1989 interview Garrett spoke further about his attitude to sleeve design:

> It wasn't about producing great paintings which I could put on the front of a record sleeve ... I was much more interested in packaging *per-se*, and packaging as part of an almost corporate identity/strategy. I was just interested in [asking] "what is the information and how can we use that to create something?"

Peter Saville Associates (PSA).[9] Peter Saville trained at Manchester Polytechnic, beginning work in the music business by designing posters and record sleeves for Tony Wilson's Manchester-based Factory Records which was begun in 1979 and named after Andy Warhol's art Factory in 1960s New York. Although frequently praised for restrained deployment of sober and established type-faces, Saville and his collaborators who have included Martyn Atkins, Ben Kelly (b.1949), photographer Trevor Key, and Brett Wickens (b.1961), are equally noted for the colour, overall minimalism of their inner and outer sleeve designs and the frequent use of object rather than person centred photography. (In the case of Key these objects are sometimes figurative sculpture which already convey the most by saying the least in the true 'classical' manner.). There is of course much indebtedness to the visual languages of the Bauhaus typographers Jan Tschichold and El Lissitzky (1890–1941). Saville's own contribution is the architectonic deployment of these and other pre-existing images on sleeves imparting an 'engineered' quality, enhanced with solid colours, quality card, perforated design elements and fine printing finishes which invite tactile and optical engagement. The fascination with a Saville sleeve is often intensified by the wilful omission or careful secretion of the title, credits and related technical information. In attempting to buy a Factory record in a shop, the consumer must either already know the imagery from press and poster advertisements, have heard and then seen it in a friend's collection or must seek enlightenment at the retail counter.

PSA's most noted designs have been for Joy Division, Orchestral Manoeuvres in the Dark, New 3.30 Order, Ultravox, and Peter Gabriel (b.1950). PSA sleeves for Factory have been seen by some as precious and dedicated works of fine design and as mass-produced commodities at one and the same time. For some they are near-parodies of conventional corporate imagery inviting the consumer to view clearly the manufacture and sale of records as part of a huge industrial operation.[10]

Saville does not work in an aesthetic, ivory tower and is always aware of the practical and commercial constraints of the record business:

> If I come up with a sleeve that gives the record company the slightest difficulty in getting their product from the factory to the shop in the north of England ...they very quickly loose interest in the design aspect. There are enormous problems in just getting pieces of paper and plastic across the country in twenty four hours in huge quantities, so if there's a sleeve that's holdings things up it has to be scrapped [11]

PSA, now at Pentagram, are beginning to see their approach to sleeve design emerge in a new generation exemplified by Johnson and Panas of Manchester.

Neville Brody.[12] In the 1980s, Neville Brody (b.1957), employed his typographic and illustrative skills for the music business, designing graphics for Stiff Records, Fetish Records, Phonogram Records and Cool Tempo Records. Experiences in magazine design and layout gave him an added edge in the search for clear modes of graphic communication. Many of Brody's designs successfully and deliberately assume a parallel position alongside the musical statements within, meshing instantly legible type and doctored photographic images, strong colouring and directional graphic symbols. Good examples of this are his work for Cabaret Voltaire on Some Bizarre/Virgin Records. The most powerful of Brody's designs appear to exist beyond the confines of the format imposed by the card or paper on which they sit as in the sleeves for *Go-Go, The Sound of Washington D.C.,* London Records, 1985. and *Just Like Every-* 3.27.a *body,* B.C. Records, 1987 for 23 Skidoo. His ability to devise new type-faces and to conjure with scale and cohesive graphic imagery, underpinned with near-architectural logic has led him to be admired and much discussed among professionals and public. As a result, a one-man show entitled *The Graphic Language of Neville Brody* was staged at the V&A Museum in 1988.   3.27.b,c

Russell Mills. Illustrator, painter and stage-set designer, Russell Mills (b.1952), translates his intricate paintings, that owe something to the art of the painter Kurt Schwitters (1887–1948) and contemporary Ian Walton (b.1950) on to the fronts of numerous LP record sleeves. With the added support of sensitive typography they complement the introverted but universally appealing sounds recorded by musicians like Brian Eno (b.1948), his brother Roger Eno, Harold Budd and David Sylvian (b.1958). In an interview with the author in 3.36 1989, Mills spoke about his sleeve designs for Brian Eno which are for him more than just a detached, professional response to a particular brief:

> It's my interpretation of feelings from that music, but there are always these reservations in that it obviously has to appeal, therefore there must be some consideration of the potential audience which is difficult because you can never know exactly what the audience might think and you don't also want to tie it down. The tightness, the restrictions of a brief come into it but they are only that it is square, it will be printed in. five colours — the limitations of printing–they're the only real limitations...

In terms of painting, Mills sees analogous processes at work when Eno and other musicians are in the recording studio. Speaking in the same interview he outlined these parallels:

They're continually following their intuition…
they have all these tools at their finger tips…its
simply a case of "what if I put this here? hmm, I
quite like that…" and then building the blocks,
putting layer upon layer, reduction, addition,
reduction, addition and that's very much the
same as making an image.

Mills is aware of an aesthetic continuity in his
sleeves for Land Records which creates a consistent, corporate message for the label informing
the consumer of its business as *'a purveyor of a
particular sensibility and integrity.'* Mills has conceded that sometimes his paintings do suffer in the
translation from the easel to the card of the sleeve:

> There are still areas of print in which you cannot
> dictate and be sure about…you look at colour in
> a *Pantone* book and you think this is how its
> going to print and just the slightest difference
> might make a huge amount of difference against
> the colours you're working with.

Other designers are also prey to the whims of
the printing process with printers occasionally
deciding to set aside specified colours with pre-
dictably disastrous results. LCO sleeve designer
Mike Dempsey (b.1944) has said:

> I've always felt printing is the fourth creative
> stage of design; if you haven't got control over it
> the job is at risk…
> Mike Dempsey in an interview with the author, 1989.

23 Envelope and Vaughan Oliver.[13] Oliver
(b.1957), working with Nigel Grierson, Christopher Bigg (b.1962) and Simon Larbalestier
(b.1962), has, under the umbrella title of 23 Envelope (established in 1981), and more recently as
V/23 created a distinctive body of original work
for the independent label 4AD founded by Ivo
3.26 Watts-Russell (b.1957). The work of 23 Envelope is
3.28.a,b centred around experimentation with old and
3.29 new type-faces, with layouts, fine calligraphy, creative photography, colour photocopies and more
recently the Quantel *Paintbox* computer system.
To do justice to the 'R&D' aspects of their work,
4AD and 23 Envelope pay considerable attention
to paper types and printing standards. 23 Envelope's designs match the clarity and gravity of
work by PSA and Brody while preserving the subtle nuances seen in the sleeve paintings of Mills
and original prints by one-time Oliver tutor Terry
Dowling (b.1946), one of his acknowledged influences. As with other, visually cohesive labels like
Factory, Land and ECM, 4AD has asked for and has
received from 23 Envelope consistent graphic

statements of quality about its special attitude to
the music it records and sells.

*The Designers Republic: Ian Anderson and
Nick Phillips.* Working with colleague Nick
Phillips (b.1962), Ian Anderson (b.1961), of
Sheffield-based Designers Republic rejects the
idea that the recording should be a major point of
reference and often chooses to give graphic focus
to ideas based on his experience of fans seen at
concerts and through business-like discussions
with musicians and record companies. A direct-
ness and honesty informs the basic typography
and imagery of Designers Republic sleeves, which
come from a respect for intuitive methods, allied
to a concentrated diligence at the drawing board
and computer screen. The whole is shot-through
with a fine thread of visual and lexical humour
inspired by titles and suggestions surrounding a
new recording.   *3.31*

Many of the mechanical, 'computer-generated' *3.32.*
letters and shapes seen in their designs are in fact *a, b*
hand-drawn, for instance, *The Heavy Metal Noise
Pollution* release from Pop Will Eat Itself carried a
microphone-toting robot which is constructed
from the initials of the group. These flat, *3.33*
autonomous san-serif 'computer' graphics (real or
pastiche), are seen frequently on electronically
generated dance records and are pendant to hip-
hop and rap graphics which tend to have a more
humanistic bias reproducing the street art of the
aerosol can.

Photography.

Photography in the realm of record-selling has
long been a merely servile, reproductive art dealing only with the presentation of a performer's
portrait. The advantages of such photo-portraits
for song-selling were evident to those in the music
business as far back as the 1840s when American
music publishers supplied their lithographers
with daguerreotypes of popular artists for study
so that faithful depictions might then be drawn
onto song-sheet stones.

From the 1930s onwards, many photo-portraits were used but maltreated because of the limits of technology and really only functioned as
'signs', giving bags a human face of a kind.[14] In the
1940s and '50s, the conventions of Hollywood-
inspired cinema showcard portraits proliferated.
These appeared in magazines and on song-sheets,
record bags and sleeves.   *3.18.a*

In the 1960s, fine-art, and fashion entered the business of rock and roll, placing a different emphasis on sleeve photography. Some of the earliest examples of creative, as opposed to reproductive photo-imagery is to be seen in photographs by Francis Wolff (d.1971), for Blue Note jazz records such as those used on *The Fabulous Fats Navarro* LP of 1956. Wolff's photographs are at once naturalistic and subjective, infusing the sleeves with an air of reflection and creativity. In the pop sphere, Beatles' LP sleeve photographs by fashion photographer Robert Freeman are early examples. Although there was a move towards freer, more expressive photography, most LP record sleeves of the late 1960s and '70s never fully questioned the notion that a recognisable photo-portrait should be there for all to see. Even when groups chose not to feature themselves on the front of a sleeve, steps were taken by designers to see that the band's equally recognisable logotype would be there to take their place and that photographs appeared prominently on the reverse. Creative adaptation of the group portrait is to be seen in the photographs of Brian Griffin (b.1948), working in the late 1970s for Echo and the Bunnymen, providing shots for the LP *Heaven up Here* designed by Martyn Atkins. Anton Corbijn, too, has worked in the territory between photo-portrait and expressive picture, most memorably with U2's *Joshua Tree* (Island Records) 1987 in conjunction with Steve Averill and the Creative Department. Ltd., Dublin. This sleeve's monumental presence stems from the designers' cinematic setting of Corbijn's desert photographs. Instances of photography acting as departure points for more advanced graphic manipulation by co-creators range from work by Rocking Russian (founded by Alex McDowell) through to the careful setting of Trevor Key's already highly imaginative camera work in the sleeves produced by PSA for the likes of OMD and New Order, through to the wistful, studied photo-constructions of Grierson and Larbalestier working with Oliver for 4AD.[15]

Classical Promotion since 1945.

If they can, they'll find a sexy 'all-teeth-and-tits' flautist, get her to churn out the 'good bits' from L'Après-Midi D'un Faune, flog it to a Saatchi's coffee ad, hype it all over Wogan, Woman's Hour and assorted chat-shows, plaster the tube with titillating posters and turn a fast buck...
Christopher Long, 'The Golden Goose', *The Music Magazine*, November 1990, p. 48.

Packaged sound recordings had, from the beginning, attracted the interest of 'serious' composers and performers. At the 1888 Handel Festival at Crystal Palace, the first ever 'live' recordings were made. A year later, Johann Brahms (1833–1897) recorded one of his Hungarian Dances, to set the seal on a trend for a sustained professional participation in the new medium. Because of technical limitations, the early recording repertoire tended more towards performances of light instrumental and vocal pieces and away from 'serious' orchestral or large-scale operatic works.

As late as 1910, with the flat disc very much the preferred format, Royal Opera House programmes were carrying advertising copy for Edison Amberol cylinders, complete with Edison's visage and lists of *'pre-eminent operatic singers'* which stated that *'Devotees of opera music can listen in comfort at their own fireside to The Edison Phonograph.'* Jostling with this and advertisements for dresses, whiskey and flowers was advertising copy for Gramophone Records supplied *'By appointment'* to five named royal personages, together with a list of recording artists and six stockists including Harrods and Selfridges.[16]

In 1931, a subscription sales campaign was established by HMV to market albums: volumes of up to 23, 78 rpm discs of 'serious' eighteenth and nineteenth-century European composers. This album schema proved to be popular, being taken up generally throughout the 1930s as popular tastes broadened to accommodate 'classics'. Separate booklets of analytical notes were included in the heavily bound and embossed paper envelopes of these releases to encourage further appreciation and sales. One example is the six disc HMV *Album Series of Complete Works* No.222. Here, Beethoven's 3rd Symphony, played by the London Philharmonic Orchestra with Sergey Koussevitsky (1874-1951), was sold with an informative booklet which included notation of the symphonic theme. The musical education of a growing body of consumers usually assumed this scholarly mode of presentation and is still to be seen in the packaging of 'serious' recordings in later decades, perhaps reaching its apogee with Deutsche Grammophon's *Archive Production Series* in the 1950s, which were issued complete with separate index cards filled with musicological data. DG has long employed restrained sleeve designs for all of its releases, utilising clear typefaces and sober period paintings, topped by the

3.11

yellow DG cartouche. This configuration first appeared in 1955 and has remained almost unchanged, even after many company realignments. Decca's *Editions de L'Oiseau-Lyre* digital *Florelegium* series of the 1980s, featuring such orchestras as The Academy of Ancient Music conducted by Christopher Hogwood (b.1941), is another example of restrained, classically informed corporate presentation. Here, thematically relevant colour reproductions of period paintings are framed by elegant, imitation letterpress fleurons which parallel title pages of the 1600s. To complete the authoritative package; pull-out, multi-lingual notes featuring photographs of performers and of associated releases are included.

Until the late 1980s, classical packaging chiefly existed to evoke authenticity, fidelity, gravity and permanence, pastoral delight or urban luxuriance. It was the product of traditionally-minded design teams, working in the knowledge that many recording artists had little say in the appearance of sleeves fronting their recordings because of long-standing contractual obligations.

In the late 1960s, companies like CBS in America presaged changes in 'serious' record packaging. They avoided cliché and down-market populism by infusing their 'classical' releases with illustrative work by the likes of Milton Glaser, (b.1929). In the 1980s, Companies like Decca , Virgin Classics and Factory with their Factory Classical label saw a need to devise fresh solutions to 'classical' sleeve design, and have therefore started to work with photographers, designers and illustrators who are stimulated by the design brief and by the possible prospect of their work outlasting that which fronts 'pop' and 'rock' sleeves. This change in attitude has resulted in the appearance of refreshing, 'pop'-inspired modes of sleeve 3.16 design and allied promotional ruses.

Bringing the LCO back to life. Working with Carroll Dempsey and Thirkell (established in 1979), Mike Dempsey and Charlotte Richardson (b.1960) have designed sleeves for the revivified London Chamber Orchestra (LCO), which is seeking to break-down ambivalent attitudes to orches-
3.15 tral music amongst younger listeners. Aided by the energetic Nigel Warren-Green and the money and freedoms granted by the Virgin Classics label, set-up by an ex-EMI classical employee, Dempsey and Richardson have gone beyond the fresh but ultimately anodyne effects of many 'wine label'

classical sleeve designs, to create a sharp profile for the LCO's vigourous recordings of Mozart (1756–1791), Vaughan Williams (1872–1958), Benjamin Britten (1913–1976), Nick Bicât (b.1949), and others. Dempsey's spirited economy for musically-related products first saw the light of day on the dust-jackets of Faber & Faber music books. He believes everyone is now sensitive to good design, so that consumer seduction can only be fully achieved through the use of original, high-quality, graphics. Care for the LCO's record packaging extends to intriguing typographical layouts which recall the four sided 'table-scores' of the late sixteenth century. The bold copy, crystal-clear imagery and multi-directional typography of the sleeves is, as per usual, applied to sundry LCO programmes, posters and press advertisements.

EMI's presentation of Nigel Kennedy as a spirited and 'fashionable' violin-toting youngster aided by frequent personal appearances on television, in record shops and in magazines, is new to the late twentieth century record buyer but is not too distant from the romantic profile afforded earlier nineteenth-century violin virtuosi like Paganini.[17]

What remains to be seen is whether the pop-like promotion of Kennedy's recordings of 'Viv' (Vivaldi) and the LCO's recordings of Mozart and Britten appeals, either to young listeners, who are often the ones whose tastes inevitably by-pass the chosen iconographic formulae discussed here, or to the other potential audience composed of mature, 'AOR' listeners, currently enjoying the no-frills, 'non-designed' packaging of acts like Ry Cooder (b.1947).[18]

The retail tale.

The 1890s. The first sound recordings were hired-out or listened to in automatic phonograph parlours which received promotion in France from posters designed by Chéret and others. The world's first retail record shop was opened by Berliner in Philadelphia in 1897. Other stores in America and Europe followed, selling discs and cylinders stored in pigeon holes behind the counter. It was common, at least in Britain to find recordings on sale in bicycle stores where mechanical expertise came in useful when dealing with troublesome phonograph and gramophone players. Many record bags at the start of the twentieth century carried graphics which advertised the presence of audition rooms at particular shops along with the availability of sundry entertainment services like the sale of theatre tickets.

Song-sheets and posters have long been used to market sound packages. (The promotion of records on song-sheets has already been briefly discussed). The Original Dixieland Jazz Band concert poster for their 1917 New York Follies appearance carries promotional copy for their Victor label record releases. In the 1930s, Paul Colin designed posters to advertise French Columbia's record releases and Adolphe Mouron Cassandre (1901–1968) executed designs for Pathé Record releases. Concert programmes have frequently carried advertisements for releases pertaining to the performers and the pieces being performed and, as has been seen, the information can even feature on concert admission tickets. Record clubs serving the domestic consumer have always been popular as promotion and sales vehicles. The first, America's RCA Victor Club, opened its books in 1934. The music and general press publish record reviews which stimulate interest in current releases and re-issues while charts of previous years are printed alongside current sales charts to renew interest in older material.[19]

HMV, Fenwick and The Browserie. In the 1930s, George Fenwick (b.1897), working for HMV studied special sales techniques seen in other retail quarters, before adapting them for the HMV chain of record shops. At the same time, he persuaded agents supplying HMV records to non-specialist shops to display them on ground floors to encourage impulse buying from consumers on their way to other departments.

Under Fenwick's guidance, new marketing initiatives employed in the HMV flagship stimulated a rapid turn-over of their stock of some thirty to forty thousand records. Extra audition rooms were fitted-out in the building and more space was given over to the display of record players. HMV encouraged recording artists to visit the shop's 'green room' to audition test recordings, a move which naturally drew autograph hunters in through the doors. HMV devoted a good deal of effort to their record player hire-purchase schemes and to the running of a busy and efficient record mail-order service. All of the staff were fully trained to run the carefully devised re-ordering system which prevented titles going 'out of stock', while a few, musically-expert staff ran the in-store information bureau.

As ever, a record heard very often meant a record sold. Tremendous efforts were made to achieve radio, live concert and record recital exposure for artists and their new releases. Record companies staged countless audio displays at exhibitions, occasionally turning to up-front marketing tactics to announce their presence by loudly playing the newest releases from chartered steam yachts sailing close to beaches, or by organising touring railway exhibitions. In the 1930s, HMV, with help from GWR did just this, fitting out and operating a 'national show train' of four coaches, with the famous HMV trademark painted on its sides. This venture was primarily intended to strengthen contacts with provincial trade representatives and retailers.[20] In 1949, a self-service racking system, possibly on the music sheet model was introduced into HMV shops which, in time, became the popular 'browserie' system of storage and display. The 'browserie' principle gave consumers the chance to search freely through racks on the shop floor, superseding the earlier method of counter storage. The first 'official' browserie appeared on a grand scale in 1955 at HMV's flagship store in London's Oxford Street.

Since the 1960s, record stores in London have been fronted by well-dressed window displays featuring graphic 'tableaux' of the latest releases. Inside the shops of the 1970s and 80s above the full display and box-racking systems are positioned large, colourful arrays of showcards, cut-outs, paintings, and long rows of empty sleeves all magnifying the graphic message of the record sleeve proper. As these window and in-store graphic displays are crucial parts of the song selling business, their formulation is not left to the whims of shop managers but are in fact devised and installed by the record companies themselves. Large stores also mount poster campaigns, an example being HMV's 1990 *Christmas Rave* campaign promoted by posters of a signed Peter Blake collage of celebrity faces in the manner of the *Sgt. Pepper* LP.

Record retailers and the influential music business figures are sent booklets, known as 'presenters', prior to the release of important new material. One such example is the ten-page, A4 format, full-colour, glossy 'presenter' designed and printed for the release of the 1990 LP *Between the Lines* by Jason Donovan (b.1968), from PWL Records. This booklet contains seven photos of Donovan, a preface, biography, discography, tour date list and a campaign account. The latter feature refers to television, press and retail promotion, to the distribution of display material for some 750 shop windows and also to the cost of television coverage in June which was to be over £400,000). Of great significance in terms of market penetration for packaged sound have been the non-print modes of television and radio, ranging from the worldwide broadcast of music videos on Music Television (MTV) through to modest but influential television shows like *Top of The Pops* and the recent use of 'oldie' 'pop' songs for commercials. Sophisticated programming of public service, and commercial radio stations ensures that a careful mix of old and new material is aired. Many stations are now experimenting with narrow casting and split frequencies offering something for everyone and so maximising listener figures.

Selling Tapes, CDs and DATs.

Experiments in sound recording during World War II, led to the commercial development of magnetic tape giving people both professional and amateur, the chance to record music easily and inexpensively. This development has been at once, an artistic liberation and a commercial curse for the music business. In recent years it has resulted in the appearance of the skull and crossed bones of the *'Home Taping Is Killing Music'* logo on many record sleeves. Perhaps in a bid to counter home taping, Warner Communications experimented in 1990 with their *Personic* system which involved the sale of customised cassettes of old hits and album tracks compiled in record shops at the request of consumers consulting catalogues of available material

Bootlegging, the illegal taping and selling of live concerts has been a serious problem for over twenty years. Bootleg tapes and records are usually packaged in simple, one-colour, low-quality paper sleeves, with a minimum amount of graphic embellishment, the very nature of its fugitive, non-professional aspect announcing its value as a rare item. Slightly different to bootlegging is the piracy of commercial studio recordings which involves the illegal duplication of copyright material. Such piracy often extends to the counterfeiting of the original, copyright packaging with a view to deceive consumers and retailers. This may be a sophisticated offset lithographic printing from new plates or the token colour-photocopy cassette inlay for pirate copies, sufficiently recognisable to signal the presence of popular recordings. A recent example of the latter is a colour photocopy inlay for a suspect copy of *Steel Wheels* by The Rolling Stones sold from a suitcase 'stall' in London's Brick Lane market. In the late 1980s, piracy, sampling, bootlegging and sophisticated packaging ploys have been seen to enter the black dance scene of Britain where so-called white label records in cheap sleeves have come to mark the presence of a commodity in limited supply. In contrast to the ubiquitous and cheap pirate cassettes, these recordings are few in number, supplying a small, relatively specialised market willing to pay £10 or £15 for each one.[21]

In the 1950s, pre-recorded, stereo reel to reel tapes were sold in flat card boxes which as a system and a commodity proved to be somewhat cumbersome and unattractive. Compact musicassettes, introduced in 1963, proved to be more convenient and quickly became one of the most popular ways of listening to pre-recorded music, outperforming the short-lived, continuous play, eight track cartridges from the USA, aimed at the English-speaking car-owner market in the 1970s. In the last decade, the inexpensive Sony Walkman personal stereo system and its imitators have ensured the survival of the cassette format. Musicassettes receive very little in the way of special packaging and are usually fronted only by diminutive LP imagery, backed by abridged, difficult-to-read text. Only occasionally will cassettes (singly or as sets) be given extensive, tailor-made inlays or be boxed to afford them greater volume and presence in shops.

Digital Commodities. Digital technology was perfected in the late 1970s, and first became available to the British consumer as the CD in 1982. In the late '80s, the imminent release of blank and pre-recorded digital audio tape (DAT), presently the smallest format for recorded music, threatened to undermine the burgeoning CD market. As a result, few record companies have experimented with the DAT format apart from Factory whose release of Joy Division's *Substance* in 1988 resulted in a small cassette package of serious charm. 1988 saw the compact disc video (CDV) become available in 12cm, 20cm and 30cm formats. It possesses packaging similar to that used for vinyl records and in fact in this field, the great graphic design challenge has been to distinguish between the two technologies in the record shop.

The reduction in the size of recording formats over the past decade has been a challenge for some designers and a problem for others. It is tackled by the adoption of the simple and globally 'legible', 'star'-silhouette. Profiles can be 'instantly' recognised at any scale of reproduction by anyone who has seen the video, watched television, or read a magazine. Notable examples of this silhouette device are those of Gabriel and Kennedy.[22] Most CDs have logotypes and recording details printed across the whole of their protective plastic surface, adding a distinguishing touch to what otherwise is a standardised product. Ironically, some of the inks used for this are thought to be capable of eating into the discs destroying the 'pure and permanent' digital information within. Graphic designer Paul Khera (b.1964), has experimented with the possibility of printing directly onto the library cases of CDs in a bid to dispense with the paper inlay but as yet his experiments have received little attention from record companies.

Trendy Diversity.

Graphics are now, in the 1990s, moving into another spontaneous, consumer-led phase and are falling into the arms of a music business keen to cultivate the 'non-designed' design. Overt stylistic precision and functionality of many '80s sleeve designs is being edged-out in favour of calligraphic individualism, painterly expressionism and calculated naivety. Examples of this are sleeve designs for The Happy Mondays' *Wrote for Luck* (1990) and Karl Denver's *Lazyitis,* designed by Manchester's Central Station Design which display some of the characteristics of the so-called scallydelia lifestyle and imagery associated with groups and clubs of England's North West. This consumer-led phase in the creation of music business graphics is very much a part of a broader, low-key movement in the graphic arts, in evidence throughout the 1980s and which embraces graffiti, psychedelic revivalism, typified by the use of floral motifs and bright colours and new wave comic book illustration.[23]

Heavy metal imagery, on the opposite flank of the business has remained rooted in a mechanistic but sensuous airbrush fantasy mode, first developed in the 1970s; it is now an indispensable presentational facet for any riff-solo-riff rock group. Heavy metal logotypes were, and still are of great

importance for the fans who take a good deal of time and trouble to sew or copy them onto denim and leather jackets as statements of allegiance.

Alongside the near-institutional graphic preoccupations of the heavy metalists and the more recent 'autographic' style, is a computer graphics mode of central stylistic importance. It proffers a 'clipped', almost bland array of fonts and forms and has grown out of the desk top publishing (DTP) movement spearheaded by Macintosh 'mice' wielded by the likes of Icon, 8vo (see their recent work for The Durutti Column), Khera at Decode Design, along with designers like Anderson, Brody and Garrett. In 1983, Apple Macintosh *3.27.c* introduced the first personal computer to make the manipulation of type on screen an easy task. This advance, alongside the introduction of high-quality laser printers, flexible type-face software packages and colour-photocopiers that can produce camera-ready images, has presented all designers with tremendous creative and presentational options. Of related interest is the Apple Macintosh *HyperCard* software system introduced in 1987, which presents a screen-based exhange of images and information. This package has been used by Voyager for their *Companion* to a CD of Beethoven's 9th Symphony. It consists of a set of *HyperCard* stacks which include a detailed graphic analysis of the music and performance styles, complete with background information on the life and times of Beethoven. Voyager are currently planning to release other *Companions* to accompany other classical and some jazz CD releases.[24] Might this kind of 'high tech' development mark the beginning of the end for paper and ink in the business of selling packaged sound?

Notes

1 Attali, J. (1985) p. 88. For Attali's strident yet largely convincing view on recorded music see pp. 87–132. Attali is somewhat critical of this commercial field, categorising it as a *'blind spectacle'* of repetition away from the animated sights and social delights of a public musical event. Yet could links between the live performers, their music and the remote audience of one, still be there to some extent in the pictorial imagery found in record packaging?

2 For accounts of the technological history of mechanical and recorded sound see: Orde-Hume, A.W.G. (1973), (1980) and (1984); BL/NSA (1988); Chew, V. K. (1981); Dearling, R. and C. (1984).

3   It was not until 1981 that guidelines for information carried on recordings for the benefit of libraries, sound archives and the public were set-out by the International Association of Sound Archives.

4   From the interview with Maurice Roach consult: BL/NSA (1989) cat. no. 85, recording: T. 10271 W.R.

5   For extensive and intelligent analysis of the art school factor in the graphics of British popular music see Walker, J. A. (1987) and Frith, S. and Horne, H. (1987).

6   On Reid see Reid, J. and Savage, J. (1987). On the vitality and variation in graphics from the late 1970s and early '80s UK single sleeve, see Greenfield, W. (1981).

7   For a first-hand account of this reversal see Rimmer, D. (1985).

8   Readhead, S. (1990) p. 38.

9   For useful insights into PSA in the early '80s see Taylor, S. (1981); Thomas, D. (1981) and Nice, J. (1984). On Saville and Pentagram see Poynor R. (1990) II.

10 For accounts of such interpretations see Frith, S. and Horne, H. pp. 136–7 and Wozencroft, J. (1988) p.56.

11 Peter Saville. Interviewed in *Designer Magazine*. (nda).

12 The best account of Brody and his work is Wozencroft, J. (1988).

13 On 23 Envelope and Vaughan Oliver see Emigre (1988) and Poynor, R. (1990) I.

14 In 1937, Decca issued special photo-portrait labels on Brunswick for stars like Bing Crosby (1903–1977) and Grace Moore. Crosby's *In a Little Hula Heaven* carries a photo of him from the film *Waikiki Wedding*. (Paramount), the catalogue of August 1937 stating: *'Souvenirs in the true sense of the word. Specially selected photographs from the films of these great artists for the label. A splendid combination of voice and the outstanding scenes from the films in which they are sung.'*

15 On pop star photography see Walker, J. A. (1987) pp.73–5. For an account of the creative activities of Grierson at 4AD see Poynor, R. (1990) I. The Smiths avoided the 'group photo' cliché by placing photographs of other stars on the front of their sleeves. See for instance the 1987 single: *I Dreamt that Somebody Loved Me* which features a smiling Billy Fury.

16 Programme for Elektra as part of the Sir Thomas Beecham Opera Season at The Royal Opera Covent Garden February 19th 1910. Enthoven Collection V&A's, Theatre Museum.

17 Issue 1 of the magazine *Classic CD* appeared with a free 'sampler' CD, stuck to a cover depicting Sir Georg Solti and the ubiquitous Kennedy. See also the 1989 Factory LP for the composer Steve Martland '... *on which he appeared sporting a flat-top haircut, half-lit and half naked, looking more like a long-lost brother of Matt and Luke Goss than a wild-haired, wild-eyed frump - the traditional composer image.'* Jeffries, S. (1990).

18 See Robert Sandall's review of Ry Cooder in concert. Sandall, R. (1990) II.

19 In January 1990, *The New Musical Express* listed some 17 music charts in its pages, including charts from the USA, soundtracks and singles of *'Twenty Years Ago'*. Large retailers like Tower Records publish in-house magazines (W.H. Smith give away their 'CD and Video *Insight Magazine* to anyone buying records in the store.) which are vehicles for reviews and general promotional imagery. Renewed interest in 'supergroups' like the Who, Led Zeppelin and Yes has prompted the music business into repackaging drives. The potency and significance of established group motifs is highlighted by the recent wrangle over Roger Dean's 'organic' logotype for a re-vitalised Yes. On the Yes logo dispute see Sandall, R. (1989) I. The fashionability of jazz in the 1980s has resulted in a fresh, eclectic approach to the packaging of this improvisatory art, albeit centred in the case of jazz on the musical personality. Surprisingly the 'cool', restrained jazz imagery of American designer Reid Miles for Blue Note Records has, in the 1980s, influenced design more in the rock and pop fields than in the new jazz scene. On Blue Note sleeve design see Kinross, R. (1990).

20 Consult an interview with George Fenwick the retired manager of the HMV shop Oxford Street. BL/NSA (1989) cat. no 23, recording: T 10032/3Y.

21 For an account of piracy and bootlegging in London see Farsides, T. (1988).

22 On the rise of the silhouette and the demise of the 'artful' sleeve see Sandall, R. (1990) III.

23 On this new trend see Murphy, D. (1990) and Rose, C. (1988).

24 *MacUser*. 24th August 1990, p. 75.

PLATE 3.1 : Four phonograph wax cylinder boxes. Average. height c.ll 0, average diameter: 6.5. Edison Amberol Record. Contains recording of Peter Dawson singing *Eileen Alannah*. 160 rpm. Des: anon. Half-tone and line-block. Pr: The Nevins Church Press, NY. c.1908. E.1273 to 1275–1988. Pasted on the lid is a label for Lloyds Cycle Stores, 6 Acre Lane Brixton. Columbia Phonograph Co. Des: anon. Colour lithography. c.1900. Private collection. Copy sets-out the types of music available from the company, namely: *'Band and orchestral selections; vocal and instrumental solo; operatic selections; stories, monologues...all the latest popular songs.'* and invites the listener to write for current lists of releases. Edison Bell Records. *The Popular Record*. Des: anon. lithography. c.1900. Private collection. *The Clarion Record*. The Premier Manufacturing Co. Ltd. London. des: anon. offset lithography. c. 1900? contains recording of Stanley Kirkby singing *When the Nightingale is Calling*. Colour lithography. E.1775, 1776–1990.

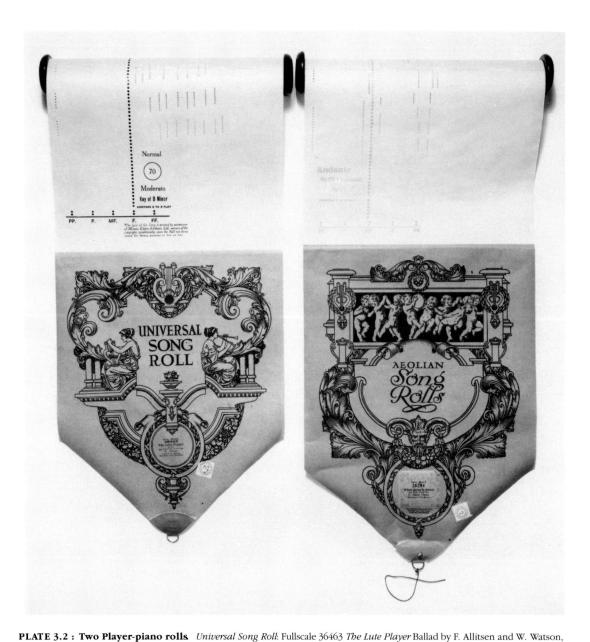

PLATE 3.2 : Two Player-piano rolls *Universal Song Roll:* Fullscale 36463 *The Lute Player* Ballad by F. Allitsen and W. Watson, played by Cyril Westbury. Des: anon. Line-block. Early twentieth century. Size of title-sheet: 34.5 x 28.5 E. 1707–1990. Title details are pasted onto one end of the roll's box. (E. 1706–1990). The roll's perforated sheet is printed with the lyric of the song together with copyright details declaring that it may not be issued for library purposes or lent on hire. *Aeolian Song Roll:* Full Scale 26294. The Aeolian Company Ltd., London and New York. *When Song is Sweet.* by G. Sans Souci, played by C. Blackmore. Des: anon. Line-block. Sold by Hickes, Reading and Gloucester, *'Noted for pianos, Gramophones, records etc.'* Early twentieth century. Size of title-sheet: 38.5 x 28.5 E.1773–1990. (Box: E.1772–1990) Note the use of the reassuringly 'classical' lyre and putti.

PLATE 3.3 : Four posters. *William Vallier; William H. Squire* (1871-1963); *Eugène Ysäye* (1858-1931); *Sir Thomas Beecham* (1879-1961). Des: anon. Lithography. 1916. Average size: 53.3 x 41.3. E.437 to 440–1916. portrait busts of Columbia's distinguished performers monochromatically rendered to harden the otherwise 'romantic' aspect of these heroes. The Columbia catalogue for 1916 uses the same poses of Beecham and Ysäye set into oval 'portrait miniature' frames on pages edged with foliate frames.

PLATE 3.4.a : Eight ten-inch 78 rpm record bags *Broadcast 12.* Machine photogravure. Des: anon. 1929–early 1932. E. 1792–1990. *Brunswick.* Des: Decca. line-block British Brunswick Ltd. London. Late 1927–1930. E. 1879–1990. In the first decades of the twentieth century, the survival of the record industry depended on the mass-purchase of radios and more especially record players and it was therefore common to see them being promoted on bags in this way. *Salon Decca* Des: Decca. Machine photogravure. 1929–c.1934. E.1877–1990. The reverse of the bag carries copy promoting Radio Paris together with some 40 solo artists and groups on Decca. *Rex Records.* Des: anon. Machine photogravure. Early 1939–1946. E.1791–1990. This design displays a number of stylistic influences including art deco air brush work, the orphism of Robert Delaunay (1885–1945) and Busby Berkeley's cinematic optical effects.

3.4.b : *The Trojan Supply Co.*, 'in-house' bag. Des: John Hassall (1868-1948)
Line-block and letterpress. Early '20s–1931. E. 1790–1990. Hassall the successful
poster artist has here produced an illustration which served as a playful motif for the
prosaic letterpress bags sold in shops as alternatives to those of the record compa-
nies. *Henry Scott* 'in-house' bag. Des: anon. Line-block and letterpress. 1928–1931.
E. 1827–1990. *Zonophone Records.* Des: Decca. Half-tone letterpress 1928–1932.
E. 1874–1990. An early example of stars' photos appearing on a record bag.
Peter Robinson Ltd., 'in-house' bag. Des: anon. Line-block and letterpress.
Late 1920s, early '30s. E. 1189–1988.

PLATE 3.5.a : 12-inch, 'in-house' 78 rpm record bag. *Holloway Stores.*
Des: anon. Line-block and letterpress. 1926–31. 31.0 x 31.9. E. 1245–1988. The design evokes the popular hotel and restaurant entertainments of the period with people dancing, not to a live orchestra but to a radio broadcast or record, which were, according to the sleeve copy, *'Better than an Orchestra'.*

PLATE 3.5.b : 12-inch 78 rpm record bag. *Essie Ackland.* Des: anon. Half-tone letterpress. 1927–8. 30.7 x 30.7. E. 1784–1990. Here the artist promotes the hardware. The reverse of the bag carries photographs of HMV record albums: multi-record sets of lengthy orchestral and operatic works.

PLATE 3.6.a : Ten-inch 78
rpm record bag Decca
Supreme Records. Des: Decca.
Machine photogravure. Early
1930s? This example possibly
c.1940–1945. E. 1236–1988.
An art deco air brush and stencil
design that owes a little to
paintings by the futurists and
vorticists.

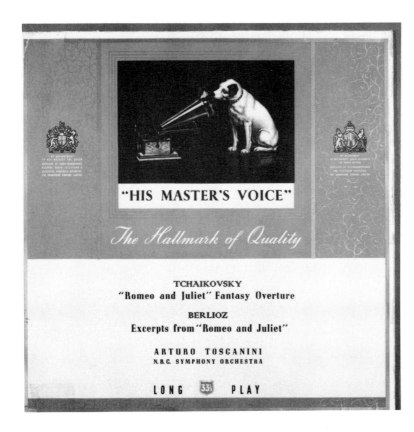

PLATE 3.6.b : 12-inch LP
record sleeve. HMV, The
Hallmark of Quality. Des: anon.
Colour half-tone and letterpress.
c. 1957–8. E. 1844–1990. The well-
worn music publishing ploy of
inserting a title into a pre-printed,
general-purpose passe-partout
frame is seen again on this formal
LP sleeve.

PLATE 3.7 : Seven-inch 45 rpm record bags.

RCA.

Des: anon. Machine photogravure c. 1954. E. 1298–1990.

Columbia Extended Play.

Des: anon. Line-block. 1950s. E. 1299, 1300–1990.

HMV.

Des: anon. Line-block. 1950s. E. 1301, 1302–1990.

This last sleeve carries the stamp of

W. G. Stores Ltd., Shepherds Bush W12.

PLATE 3.8 : Two ten-inch 33rpm record bags, and seven-inch, 45 rpm record and bag.

Columbia/EMI. Des: anon. c. 1959. Line-block. E. 1873–1990. The reverse carries copy advertising LPs and EPs together with a paragraph on the advantages of microgroove recordings.

His Master's Voice for the Tops in Pops. Des: anon. Line-block c.1959. E. 1783–1990.

Columbia/EMI. Des: anon. Line-block. c.1959. E. 1786, 1787–1990.

These three designs reflect the record industry's growing interest at this date in the young, increasingly affluent record buyer, whose independence was often expressed in listening to records at home on portable players and at party dances.

PLATE 3.9 : 12-inch LP record sleeve. *The Who Live at Leeds,* complete with inserts including *The Who Maximum R 'n' B* Marquee poster (E. 846–1985). Des: Graphreaks. Offset lithography. Polydor Records Ltd. Pr. & manufactured: MacNeill Press Ltd., London. 1970. E. 1216–1988. Guitarist Pete Townshend (b.1945) and manager Kit Lambert brought a self-conscious pop art sensibility to the music, actions and packaging of The Who *'the first pop art band'*. Dada and later Pop Art used media and conventions of the fine art world to elevate and enervate mundane and transient artifacts. Here, within a sleeve masquerading as a bootleg, facsimiles of written and printed paper ephemera generated by The Who's live performances are given an air of permanent significance as art objects in the manner of Marcel Duchamp (1887–1968). At another level, they are documents exposing the mechanics of the rock spectacle.

PLATE 3.10 : 12-inch 'gatefold' LP sleeve. *Led Zeppelin III.* Des: Zacron. Offset lithography. Atlantic Recording Corp., USA. Polydor Ltd. Pr. & manufactured: E. J. Day Group Ltd., London and Bedford. 1970. E. 1195–1988. Fragmentary 'scrap-book' images induce viewers to 'graze' around a sleeve that relegates photos of the four group members to the back. The rotating wheel was originally intended to allow viewers to 'dial-up' icons representing the interests of Jimmy Page (b.1944), *et al.* This consumer participation adds an absorbing new dimension to the product.

**PLATE 3.11 : Six 12-inch Blue Note LP record
sleeves.** Each c.31.5 x 31.3. *GO!* Dexter Gordon
(1923–1990) Des: Reid Miles. Photo: Francis Wolff
(d.1971). Offset lithography. 1962.

*The Ornette Coleman Trio at the
"Golden Circle" Stockholm Volume I.*
(Coleman b. 1930). Des: Reid Miles.
Photo: Francis Wolff Offset lithography. 1965.

The Real McCoy. McCoy Tyner (b.1938).
Des: Reid Miles. Photo: Francis Wolff.
Offset lithography 1967.

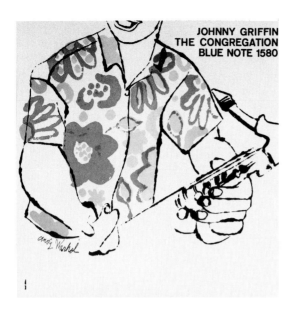

The Congregation. Johnny Griffin (b.1928).
Des: Andy Warhol (1928–1987) & Reid Miles.
Offset lithography. 1984 re-issue of original 1957 release.

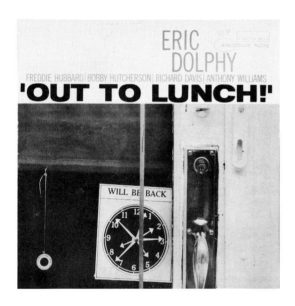

Out to Lunch! Eric Dolphy (1928–1964).
Des & photo: Reid Miles. Offset lithography. 1964.

The Fabulous Fats Navarro (1923-1950). Volume I. Des: Reid
Miles. Photo: Francis Wolff. 1956. The effortless
sophistication of the jazz musicians recording with Blue
Note in the 1950s and '60s found a visual metaphor in the
sleeve designs of Reid Miles. His penchant for cropped
lettering, photographs and even cropped Warhol drawings
has resulted in such sleeves being regarded by nearly
everyone as *the* face of jazz on record.

PLATE 3.12 : Two 12-inch LP sleeves. ECM Records. *Dis.* Jan Garbarek (b.1947). ECM 1093.
Cover photo Franco Fontana. Layout Barbara Wojirsch (b.1939/40). Offset lithography. 1977. E. 1648–1990.
Accélération. Hans Koch, Martin Schütz and Marco Käppeli. ECM 1357.
Des & photo: Dieter Rehm (b. 1957/8). Offset lithography. 1987. E. 1635–1990.
Recordings by European 'chamber jazz' musicians on Manfred Eicher's ECM label were packaged in sleeves that consistently
summed-up the rarified, controlled expressionism of their music. This was most often accomplished with photographs of the
natural environment which were approximate visual equivalents of the acoustic, meditative sounds within.
New Age sleeve design has been much influenced by ECM's approach which in turn ultimately owes something to the
photographs of Pete Turner for Creed, the CTI jazz label.

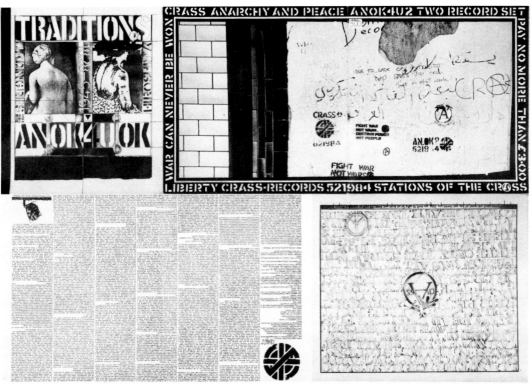

PLATE 3.13 : 12-inch double LP poster-sleeve and original interior collage. *Stations of the Cross/Crass.* Crass.
Des: Gee Vaucher (b. 1945), and Penny Rimbaud. Offset lithography. Crass Records. 1979. c.62.2 x 93.3. E. 1208–1988.
The Crass collective's multi-media promotion of personal expression and autonomy found favour with a large sector of
Britain's youth in the late 1970s and early '80s rejecting the escapism of 'pop' and the clichéd pleasures of rock. With a late 1960s
bias towards self-generated messages and imagery of near-tribal significance, Crass welded together disparate social comments
with intentionally abrasive sounds and pictures. The graphic messages of Crass appeared on walls as often as on sleeves and were
there to 'sell' an alternative system of attitudes and offer a binding ritual focus. Crass Records encouraged young groups to
submit their own music and graphics for pressing, printing and release. The material received was issued as two compilation LPs.

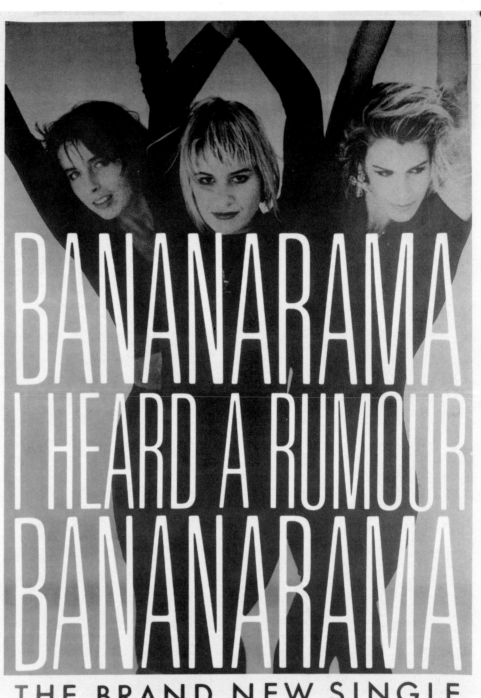

PLATE 3.14 : Poster. I Heard a Rumour. *Bananarama.*
Des: anon. Offset lithography. London Records. 1987. 154.0 x 103.6. E. 469–1988.
A poster promoting two, 45 rpm single formats which would have probably occupied one of the
thousands of illegal inner-city sites across the UK. The sensuous nature of this highly successful all-woman
vocal group is here tempered by the dominant typographical message.

PLATE 3.15 : Four 12-inch LP record sleeves. The London Chamber Orchestra.

LCO 1. This conveys the sharpness and breadth of Mozart's musical vision.

LCO 2. This is a condensation of imagery associated with the pastoralism of English orchestral pieces: .

An oak leaf and a small portion of airbrush 'sky' symbolising the distant lark. Note the facsimile signatures.

LCO 3. This uses an egg, red paint, gold leaf and a glass marble as symbols of the seasons.

LCO 4. (the reverse). Des: Mike Dempsey (b.1944) & Charlotte Richardson (b.1960), Carroll Dempsey

and Thirkell. Offset lithography. Virgin Classics. 1989. E. 1851,1850,1849,1848–1990.

PLATE 3.16 : CD inlay card and two CD libretto booklets. For each: picture research: Leander Shrimpton (b.1962), des: Richard Bonner Morgan (b.1964), art direction Ann Bradbeer (b.1959). Each c.12.0 x 27.

A Midsummer Night's Dream. Britten. LSO. (double CD inlay). Photo: Erich Auerbach, The Hulton-Deutsch Collection. 1960. Offset lithography. The Decca Record Company Ltd. Printed in West Germany. 1990. V&A Museum. This digitally re-mastered recording (ADD), was first released in 1967.

Albert Herring. Britten. ECO. (Double CD booklet). Photo from the BBC Hulton Picture Library, 1949. Offset lithography. The Decca Record Company Ltd. 1987. V&A Museum. First released in 1964.

Billy Budd. Britten. LSO. (Triple CD libretto booklet). Decca. Photo from BBC Hulton Picture Library. Offset lithography. 1989. V&A Museum. First released 1968. On the back of each CD is a small reproduction of the original 1960s sleeve.

PLATE 3.17.a : Poster. *Clara Butt.* Des: anon.
Offset lithography. Columbia Records.
c.1916. 56.0 x 39.6 E. 460–1916.
The aloofness and near arrogance of Columbia's black
and white portraits of Beecham *et al* are absent in this
softer, more sensuous image conveyed by the arctic
fox-fur, delicate skin tones and roses, yet an air of
professional composure is maintained.
The 'exclusive' nature of operatic recordings
at this time is here illustrated by the graded
prices at the poster's lower edge.

PLATE 3.17.b : Poster. *Claire Waldoff.*
Des: Hans Rewald. Offset lithography.
Before 1933. 140.3 x 95.9. E. 359–1932.
In contrast with the naturalistic portrait of Clara Butt,
illustrator Rewald has here chosen to communicate the
personality of Waldoff and advertise her recordings
on Parlophon and Odeon in a manner just short of
unflattering caricature.

PLATE 3.18.a : Two ten-inch LP record sleeves and 12-inch LP record sleeve. *Satchmo Serenades.* Louis Armstrong. (1901-1971). Des: anon. Half-tone letterpress. Brunswick. 1954. 25.4 x 25.5. Private Collection. *Collectors' Classics, Vol. 4. Bing Crosby.* Des: anon. Machine photogravure and letterpress. Brunswick. 1956. 25.4 x 25 5. Private Collection. Like Crosby, Armstrong began his recording career in the 1920s and became a star of stage, radio and screen cutting through racial preferences with his popular material couched in jazz terms. Armstrong's familiar visage is here treated to a bizarre setting of motifs of no particular import which derive from the modernism of post-war American graphics. This desire to signify modernity often occurs in music business sleeve designs and posters when current stylistic awareness in art departments hinders the production of more empathetic images. The work of concert, recording, radio and film star Crosby dominated the American popular music field for half a century. This compilation attests the continuing viability of selling the 'collected works'. The photo and autograph formula recalls that of the nineteenth-century sheet-music of adored, money-spinning artists.

PLATE 3.18.b : *Thursday's Child.* Eartha Kitt (b.1928). Des: anon. Offset lithography. HMV. 1956. 31.1 x 31.3. Private Collection. The simple but resonant photo-portrait of Eartha Kitt here creates and imparts a seductive demeanour.

PLATE 3.19 : Two 12-inch LP 'gatefold' record sleeves.

Sgt. Pepper's Lonely Hearts Club Band. The Beatles. Des: M. C. Productions & The Apple staged by Peter Blake (b.1932)
& Jann Haworth. Photo: Michael Cooper. Offset lithography. Parlophone EMI.

Pr. & manufactured: Garrod & Lofthouse Ltd., 1967. E. 577–1985.

Now the most celebrated 'underground' record and sleeve design ever issued, *Sgt. Pepper* was originally mixed for mono
release and was nearly sold (at Epstein's suggestion), in a plain cover to avoid any possible litigation. The design was conceived
as a montage celebration of the celebrity, calling upon the pop art–fine art talents of Blake and Howarth to inject a certain
monumentality into what may otherwise have been a work of lesser moment.

The record is not strictly a concept album like those with strong lyrical or narrative content which followed in the 1970s,
yet the special unity and self-importance achieved through track linkage, carefully chosen popular and counter-cultural
iconography does impart an operatic air of consistent thematic treatment.

Included in the package was a separate coloured 'cut-out' sheet of moustache and sergeant stripes,
an idea first aired in *Ark,* The Royal College of Art magazine.

Their Satanic Majesties Request. The Rolling Stones. Des: & photo: Michael Cooper.

(Back cover illus: Tony Meeviwiffen). Offset lithography. Decca. Pr: Robert Stare, England. 1967. E. 576–1985.

The central image is printed on a faceted sheet of plastic to create a pseudo three-dimensional effect.

The set was built by the Rolling Stones, Michael Cooper and Archie at Pictorial Productions, Mount Vernon, NY.

It is a direct ripost to the Peter Blake *Sgt. Pepper* sleeve for the Beatles, released in the same year.

This design, together with the music within illustrates how even a group of such a well-defined self-image as the
Stones could not resist experimenting with the ubiquitous psychedelic and eastern influences of the time.

PLATE 3.20 : Poster. *Burning of the Midnight Lamp.* The Jimi Hendrix Experience.
Des: 'P.' Screenprint in three colours on silver foil. Track Records. 1968. 74.2 x 49.6. E. 34–1968.
A poster of originality, typographical understatement and technical innovation which perfectly encapsulates
the fluidity, prismatic play and licence of Hendrix recordings in a unconscious, un-tutored way,
so often absent in many other psychedelic rock posters of this date.

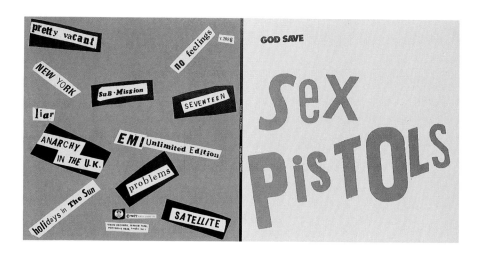

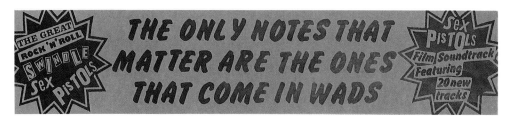

PLATE 3.21 : 12-inch LP record sleeve proof and two strip posters *God Save Sex Pistols*. The Sex Pistols.

Des: Jamie Reid (b.1947). Offset lithography. Virgin Records Ltd. 34.2 x 64.1.

V&A Museum's Theatre Museum, Rock and Pop archive, S. 717–1990.

A trial proof for the LP eventually issued under the title *Never Mind the Bollocks Here's the Sex Pistols*. The LP which

is in essence a 'best of' compilation, was rush released in November 1977 in a bid to dampen sales of imported recordings.

A high number of proofs were associated with this release to ensure that the complex overlays and use of temperamental

fluorescent inks (particularly yellow which is prone to spoiling), meshed as Reid had intended.

The Only Notes That Matter and *While Stocks Last*. Des: Jamie Reid. Offset lithography.

15.0 x 70.0 and 25.5 x 63.4. V&A's Theatre Museum, Rock and Pop Archive. S. 718, 719–1990.

Issued to promote the LP *The Great Rock and Roll Swindle* film soundtrack released in advance of the film itself.

The sleeve is a tour de force from Reid and Trevor Key, and is here supported by fluorescent banners in the manner of the

first LP. The film was made as an assemblage of ten post-facto 'lessons' on how to succeed in the music business.

The first four of these lessons were: 1. *How to Manufacture Your Group*; 2. *Establish the Name Sex Pistols*; 3. *Sell the Swindle*;

4. *Do Not Play, Don't give the Game away*. The Sex Pistol's Music, McLaren's subversive management style and Reid's DIY

graphics profoundly influenced hundreds of emergent punk bands, independent labels and young designers in the late 1970s.

PLATE 3.22 :. Poster. *Never Mind The Bollocks Here's The Sex Pistols.* Des: Jamie Reid & John Varnom. Offset lithography. Virgin Records Ltd. Courtesy of Kasper de Graaf at Assorted Images. 99.5 x 65.0. E. 839–1985. Arranging the graphic images of the singles sleeves as a collage, this is, in effect, a summation of Reid's early work for the Pistols. Reid's 'guerrilla graphics' had the desired effect of stunning a complacent music business and record-buying public sated by a preponderance of airbrush illustration and glamorous group photography.

PLATE 3.23.a : 12-inch LP sleeve. *Peter Gabriel 1.*
Des: Hipgnosis. Offset lithography. Charisma Records Ltd.
Pr: James Upton Ltd., England. 1977. E.1186–1988.
This, Gabriel's first solo LP shows a plain-faced singer in
the front seat of a car on a wet and grey day. The careful
hand-tinting of the photograph and the super-realist
presentation of the rain droplets creates a new actuality
which transmutes the otherwise mundane photograph into
an unsettling confection.

3.23.b : 12-inch LP record sleeve. *Squeeze.* Squeeze.
Des: Nick Marshall. Art direction: Michael Ross
Mr. Universe photo: George Greenwood.
Offset lithography. A&M Records Ltd.
Pr: CMCS Print & Colour Ltd. 1978. E. 371–1980.
This partly artful, partly funny, Pop Art and Reid
inspired design fronting the LP of new wave pop group
Squeeze, perfectly captures the spirit of their
serio-comic song-writing and performance.

3.23.c : 12-inch 45 rpm single record sleeve.
Better Must Come. Junior C. Reaction.
Des: Stephen Horse. Offset lithography.
Chrysalis Records Ltd. 1986. E. 1198–1988.
In spite of claims in the 1970s that there were supply
problems with paper and vinyl, the 12-inch single format
was introduced to give songs a higher marketing profile.
Songs were extended and re-mixed to create a 'new'
product that 'improved' overall sales figures.
An additional benefit of the format was that the widely-
spaced microgrooves on a large vinyl platter offered finer
sound reproduction. Here, like some film or television
programme title the artist's name is projected away
from the housing blocks, and seems to break-
out of the sleeve's grey world.

129

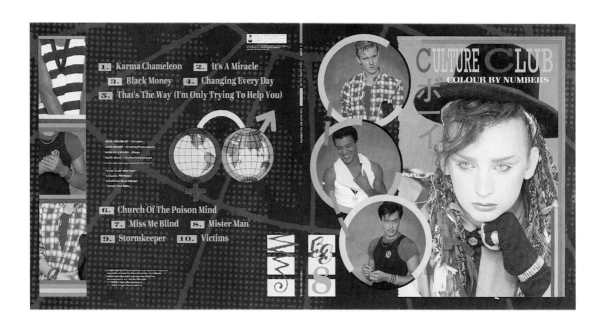

PLATE 3.24 : 12-inch LP record sleeve proof and picture disc proof. *Colour By Numbers.* Culture Club.
Des: Malcolm Garrett (b.1956). Photo: Jamie Morgan. Offset lithography. Virgin Records Ltd. 35.1 x 64.0. E. 1323, 1322–1990
Here, Garrett combines the photogenic androgyny of lead singer Boy George (b.1961) and conventional 'pin-up'
characteristics of group members with pastel coloured curvelinear forms against a dark globe to create a busy design of subtle,
rotating undercurrents. Fusion of pictures and records first appeared in 1920s America.
Frequently released today as 'limited edition' promotional artifacts, such discs are purchased by fans
and collectors in spite of them being inferior, in audio terms, to plain discs.
Note that the sleeve proof carries the colours red gold and green on the female, male and asexual
symbols in a response to echo the rasterfarian colours featured in the song *Karma Chameleon*.

PLATE 3.25 : Poster. For the LP *True Blue*. Madonna (b.1958). Des: anon. Offset lithography. WEA/Sire. 1986. 152.3 x 101.6. E. 152–1987. In this poster, Madonna projects a seductive profile on a poster which echoes the imagery of the commodity being sold: the LP. More recently Madonna has projected an assertive, more liberated stance on stage, in video and in her poster and sleeve imagery. This she has laced with her interest in Christian iconography and her established, Marilyn Monroe-like sexuality.

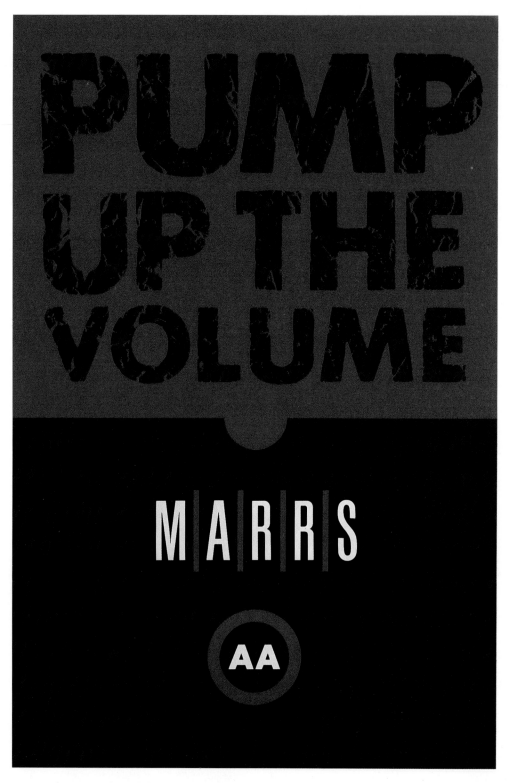

PLATE 3.26 : Poster. For the single *Pump Up The Volume*. M/A/R/R/S. Offset lithography. 4AD 1987.
152.1 x 101.3. E. 356–1989. Unlike the *True Blue* poster which sustains and extends Madonna's persona with a view to
encouraging sales of all her recordings, this poster presents a deliberately objective, faceless promotion of a unique,
collaborative single. *Pump Up the Volume* was an aural collage of musical samples taken from some 30 recordings laid
upon an existing piece by 4AD artists Colourbox and A. R. Kane. Its tremendous popularity (it topped the 12-inch
single sales chart for 1987), resulted in the anonymity of its original, 'white label' aspect being replaced by the more
distinctive though still non-human, typographical 'persona' seen here.

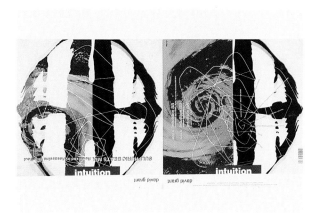

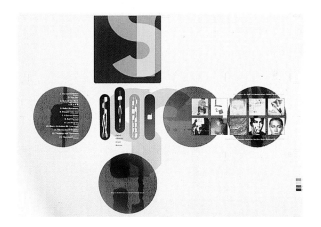

PLATE 3.27.a : 12-inch double 45 rpm single record sleeve. *Go-Go. The Sound of Washington D.C.* Des: Neville Brody (b.1957). Offset lithography. London Records. 1985.

PLATE 3.27.b : 12-inch 45 rpm single record sleeve. *Intuition. Sulphuric Beats Mix.* David Grant. Des: Neville Brody and Tony Cooper. Offset lithography. Fresher Records. 1988.

PLATE 3.27.c : Proof of CD box inlays. *Gruppo Musicale.* Ryuichi Sakamoto. Des: Neville Brody, Tony Cooper and Cornel Windlin. Offset lithography. Midi Records. 1988. 40.5 x 53.6.

In the late 1980s, Brody began to allow Macintosh-aided design methods to take him away from the grand and vivacious manual gesture seen in his early work and on towards a cooler, less-complex rendition of image and message.

PLATE 3.28.a : Poster. *Modern English*. Des: Vaughan Oliver (b.1957). Offset lithography. 4AD. 1982. c.30 x 21. E. 332–1989. Modern English were one of the first bands to be released on the 4AD label, set-up in late 1979 by Ivo Watts-Russell under the auspices of Beggars Banquet Records. Oliver designed Modern English record sleeves and this poster before working full-time for 4AD in 1983.

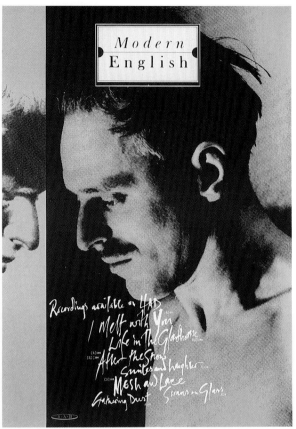

PLATE 3.28.b : Poster. *Victorialand*. The Cocteau Twins. Des: Vaughan Oliver, photo: Nigel Grierson. (23 Envelope). Offset lithography. 4AD. 1986. c.30 x 21. E. 324–1989. Here on the poster (and again on the record sleeve), Oliver has isolated Grierson's photograph to present it as an image on a gallery wall. This contrasts with most of their designs for the Cocteau Twins at this date which comprised textural photographs running across the entire surface of the sheet or sleeve.

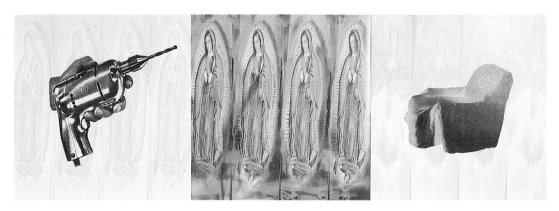

PLATE 3.29 : Twelve-inch LP record sleeve, inner sleeve and fold-out triptych. *Joy 1967-1990*. Ultra Vivid Scene.
Des: Vaughan Oliver/v23, *'(With thanks to the Ralske Archives and Mr. Baker at IQ.)'*. Offset lithography 4AD. 1990.
31.3 x 31.4. 30.5 x 30.9 and 30.9 x 91.0. E. 1738 to 1740–1990. Oliver has used the Quantel computer system to realise
an extraordinary juxtaposition of icons held together in a well-balanced layout of luxuriant colour.

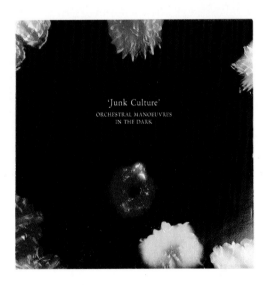

PLATE 3.30 : Four record sleeves. 12-inch single record sleeve. *Stereo/Porno.* Vermorel. Des: Peter Saville Associates (PSA). Offset lithography. A Factory Record. 1988. E. 2264 to 2266–1990.

12-inch LP record sleeve. *Technique.* New Order. Des: PSA. Photo: Trevor Key. Offset lithography. Factory Communications. 1989. E. 2267 to 2269–1990.

12-inch LP record sleeve. *So.* Peter Gabriel. Des: Brett Wickens (b.1961) with PSA. Charisma Records Ltd.,1986. E. 2270–1990.

12-inch LP record sleeve. *Junk Culture.* Orchestral Manoeuvres in the Dark. Des: PSA. Photo: Richard Haughton. Virgin Records Ltd., 1984. E. 2271 to 2273–1990.

'I'm not automatic – designs evolve. Visually there are discussions with management, the record company and the band as to what the sleeve is going to be and a decision is taken. With New Order, I have to decide what it's going to be, and the band leave us to get on with it. I express something that I'm interested in. This year, designing Technique, I was interested in shopping for antiques.' Peter Saville (b.1955) interviewed in the PSA Tenth Anniversary supplement. *Music Week* (1990) p. 6.

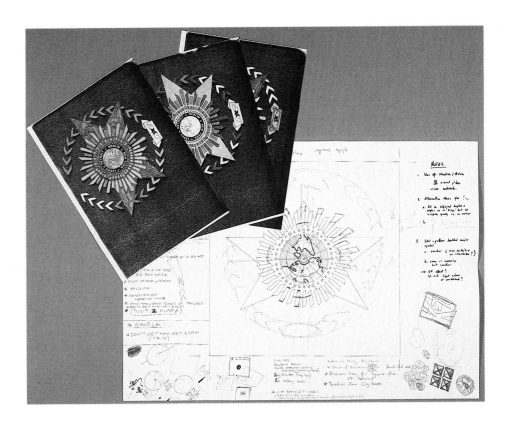

PLATE 3.31 : 'First thought' sketch, trial A4 photocopy colourways and completed sleeve artwork. *One Thousand Years of Trouble.* Age of Chance. Des: The Designers Republic: Ian Anderson (b.1961) and Nick Phillips (b.1962). Pencil, ball-point pen, felt marker and wash. 1987. 41.7 x 59.1. E. 843–1990 and E. 841, 844, 845–1990. Felt marker, tracing sheet, acetate and PMT (photomechanical transfer). 50.6 x 75.0. E. 855–1990. The images in this design strive to present 'the world' of the Age of Chance picked-out of The Designers Republic studio file on the group. This 'world' was one of loudness and a confused mix of slogans and images. Just as the imagery of the Age of Chance singles should hold the viewer's interest for three to four minutes, so this LP record sleeve design should sustain itself for 20 or more minutes.

3.32.a : 12-inch LP record sleeve. *One Thousand Years of Trouble.* Age of Chance. Des: The Designers Republic. Offset lithography. Virgin Records Ltd. 1987. E. 789–1990. The finished sleeve constructed from the elements seen in plate 3.31 and constitutes a sort of 'passport' to the world of the Age of Chance.

PLATE 3.32.b : 12-inch single record sleeve. *House Arrest. Burn Down the House Mix.* Krush. Des: The Designers Republic. Offset lithography with spot varnish. Fon Records 1987. E. 746-1990. In the late 1980s, the widespread appropriation of 'designer labels' like Gucci for use on imitation goods and as fashion statements for the young extended to include the logos of car manufacturers. The rap duo The Beastie Boys and their fans took to wearing 'VW' badges as pendants, taken from parked Volkswagen cars. The use here of the Mercedes Benz symbol was in part inspired by a shirt print of the logo and is a deliberate ploy to take Krush one degree higher in the exclusivity stakes.

PLATE 3.33 : Extended-play special cassette single and package, shaped picture disc and Seven-inch extended play gatefold record sleeve. *Very Metal Noise Pollution.*

PWEI (Pop Will Eat Itself). Des: The Designers Republic. Offset lithography. RCA. 1989.

Cassette package: 18.2 x 18.2. E. 833 to 837–1990. Picture disc diameter: 28.3. E. 728, 729–1990.

Gatefold: E. 815–1990. Just three of the various formats

PLATE 3.34 : Three compact disc catalogues. *Decca Ovation Catalogue, mid-price CDs.* Private collection. *Decca Compact Disc Catalogue. 1988-89.* E. 1319–1990. *Decca Compact Disc Catalogue. Spring 1989.* E. 1320–1990. Des: Decca. Offset lithography. Average size: 29.8 x 21.0. A seventeenth century copper engraving and a nineteenth century wood-engraving provide the basis for these 'post-modern' designs, redolent with authority, taste and learning.

PLATE 3.35 : Compact disc catalogue. *Luciano Pavarotti.* (b.1935) on Compact Disc.

Des: Decca. Photo: Christian Steiner. Offset lithography. 29.5 x 20.9. c.1989. E.1318–1990.

Within are details of Pavarotti's CD recordings on Decca, accompanied by small reproductions of the respective inlay designs.

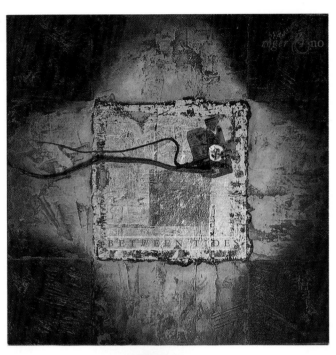

PLATE 3.36 : 12-inch LP record sleeve, Three promotional stickers and compact disc and library case.
Between Tides. Roger Eno. Des: Russell Mills (b.1952) and Dave Coppenhall. (The original cement, acrylic
and collage painting by Mills: c.60 x 60). Photo: Jeff Veitch. Offset lithography. Land Records. 1988.
E. 1590-1990. Stickers: 8.6 x 12.0. E. 1590 (1), (2), (3)–1990. Disc diameter: 12.
Case opens to: 12.4 x 27.5. E. 1610 to 1611-1990.The painting emerged after many discussions with
Roger Eno. Mills, (appointed art director/consultant of Land Records in 1988), became so
involved in the music that he even selected the titles for a majority of the compositions.
The painting explores the confluence of nature, science and religion.

REFERENCES

Arts Council of Great Britain (1986). *Eye Music. The Graphic Art of New Musical Notation*. London. An exhibition booklet.

Attali, J. (1985). *Noise. The Political Economy of Music*. Trans. Brian Massumi. Theory and History of Literature, Vol. 16. Manchester University Press. (1st pub. as *Bruits*, 1977).

Bailey, D. (1980). *Improvisation. Its Nature and Practice in Music*. Moorland Publishing in association with Incus Records, Ashbourne, Derbyshire.

Bailey, P. ed. (1986). *Music Hall: The Business of Pleasure*. Popular Music in Britain Series, Open University Press. Milton Keynes.

Bartsch (1984). *The Illustrated Bartsch*, 13. German Masters of the Sixteenth Century. Walter L. Strauss, Arabis Books, NY.

BL/NSA (1988). *Revolutions in Sound. A Celebration of 100 Years of the Gramophone*. British Library National Sound Archive, London. An exhibition booklet.

BL/NSA (1989). *Developments in Recorded Sound*. The British Library National Sound Archive, London. A catalogue of oral history interviews.

Blumenthal, A. R. (1980). *Theater Art of the Medici*. University Press of New England. An exhibition catalogue.

BMYB (1990) *The British Music Year Book*. Andrew Stewart ed., Rhinegold Publishing Ltd. London.

Bratton, J. S. ed. (1986). *Music Hall Performance and Style*. Popular Music in Britain Series. Open University Press, Milton Keynes.

Brody, E. (1988). *Paris. The Musical Kaleidoscope, 1870-1925*. Robson Books Ltd. (1st pub. in the USA, 1987).

Buxton, D. (1983). Rock Music, The Star System and the Rise of Consumerism. *Telos* 57. (Reprinted in *On Record*. Frith and Goodwin (1990) pp. 427–440.)

Carr, R., Case, B. and Dellar F. (1986). *The Hip. Hipsters, Jazz and the Beat Generation*. Faber & Faber, London.

Chambers, I. (1988). *Popular Culture. The Metropolitan Experience*. Studies in Communication. John Fiske gen. ed., Routledge. London. (1st pub. 1986).

Chew, V. K. (1981). *Talking Machines*. The Science Museum HMSO, 2nd edition.

Cooper, J. (1983). *The Rise of Instrumental Music and Concert Series in Paris, 1828–1871*. Studies in Musicology, no. 65. George Buelow series ed., UMI Research Press, Ann Arbour Michigan.

Coover, J. (1985). *Music Publishing, Copyright and Piracy in Victorian England*. Mansell Publishing Ltd., London.

Coral, L. (1967). A John Playford Advertisement. [Harley 5936/421, Bagford Coll.] *Royal Musical Association Research Chronicle*, 5. pp. 1–12.

Csida, J. and Bundy, J. (1978). *American Entertainment. A Unique History of Popular Show Business*. A Billboard book. Watson-Guptill Publishers. NY.

Cutler, C. (1985). What is Popular Music? in *Popular Music Perspectives* 2. pp. 3–12. The International Association for the Study of Popular Music, 2nd international conference held in Reggio Emilia, 1983

Darling, A. and Glanvill, R. (1989). Contract what Contract? *City Limits*, March 16th–23rd, pp. 12–14.

Dart T. (1975). *The Interpretation of Music*. Hutchinson, London. (1st pub. 1954).

Eisenberg, E. (1988). *The Recording Angel. Music, Records and Culture from Aristotle to Zappa*. Picador, London.

Emigre (1988). *Emigre Magazine* 9. Berkeley California.

Farsides, T. (1988). Putting the Boot in. *City Limits*, June 16th–23rd, pp. 12–15.

Fiske, R. (1973). *English Theatre Music in the Eighteenth Century*. Oxford University Press, London.

Fraenkel, G. S. (1968). *Decorative Music Title Pages. 201 examples from 1500–1800*. Dover Publications Inc., NY.

Frith, S. (1978). *The Sociology of Rock*. From the series Communication and Society, Jeremy Tunstall series ed., Constable, London.

Frith, S. and Horne, H. (1987). *Art into Pop*. Methuen, London.

Frith, S. (1990). Frankie Said: But what did they mean? in *Consumption, Identity and Style*, Alan Tomlinson ed., Routledge. London, 1990. pp. 172–185.

Grant, S. *et al* (1989). Articles on hype. *Time Out*, March 8th–15th, pp. 16–21.

Greenfield, W. (1981). For Singles Only. *Print*. (America's graphic design magazine), September-October.

Grushkin, P. D. (1987). *The Art of Rock. Posters from Presley to Punk*. Abbeville Press, NY.

The Hafler Trio (1986). *The Sea Org*. Booklet issued with ten inch, 45 rpm record, *The Sea Org*. Touch 5.

Haill, C. (1981). *Victorian Illustrated Music Sheets*. V&A Museum, HMSO, London.

Handel/NPG (1985). *Handel. A Celebration of his Life and Times, 1685–1759*. London. National Portrait Gallery exhibition catalogue.

Hindley, C. H. (1970). *The Life and Times of James Catnach (late of Seven Dials) Ballad Monger*. Welwyn Garden City. (1st pub. 1887).

Hirsch, P. M. (1972). Processing Fads and Fashion. *American Journal of Sociology* 77. University of Chicago Press. (Reprinted in *On Record*. Frith and Goodwin (1990) pp.127–139.)

Imeson, W.E. (1912). *Illustrated Music Titles*, London.

Jefferies, S. (1990). Burning at the Stave. *The Guardian*, October 25th, p. 27.

Kauffer, E. M. (1924). *The Art of the Poster. Its Origin, Evolution and Purpose*. Cecil Palmer, London.

King, A. H. (1979). *Four Hundred Years of Music Printing*. British Library. London.

Kinross, R. (1990). Cool Clear and Collected. *Eye, The International Review of Graphic Design* 1, vol. 1. pp. 72–82.

Krummel. D.W. (1986). Publishing and Printing of Music. *The New Grove Dictionary of Music*, Vol. 3, H.W Hitchcock and Stanley Sadie eds., Macmillan, London.

Leppert, R. (1988). *Music and Image: Domesticity, Ideology and Socio-Cultural Formation in Eighteenth-Century England*. Cambridge University Press.

Malone, P. (1990). Stick 'em up. *The Evening Standard Magazine*, February, pp. 42–6.

Martin, M. (1987). The Case of the Missing Woodcuts, *Print Quarterly* vol. IV no. 4. pp. 343–361.

McAfee, A. (1988). Lord of the Flies. *The Evening Standard*, June 27th.

Middleton, R. (1990). *Studying Popular Music*. Open University Press, Buckingham.

Morley, S. (1989) The Art of the London Hit Men. *The Times*, December 16th, p. 27.

Murphy, D. (1990). Local Colour. *Creative Review*, June 1990, pp. 33–6.

Music Week (1990). FAC 229! The *Music Week* Factorial, *Music Week*, July 15th, 1989.

Nice, J. (1984). Perfect Stylistic Attitude. *Magazine*, Glasgow University, May to December.

O'Hagen, S. (1990). Music and Money Make a Field Day. *The Sunday Correspondent*, April 29th.

Ord-Hume, A. W. J. G. (1973). *Clockwork Music: An Illustrated History of Mechanical Musical Instruments*. Allen & Unwin.

Ord-Hume, A. W. J. G. (1980). *Musical Box: A History and Collector's Guide*. Allen and Unwin.

Ord-Hume, A.W.J.G. (1984). *Pianola, the History of the Self-Playing Piano*. George Allen & Unwin.

Paulson, R. (1989). *Hogarth's Graphic Works*. 3rd revised edition. The Print Room, London.

Pearsall, R. (1973). *Victorian Popular Music*. David & Charles, Newton Abbot.

Pearsall, R. (1975). *Edwardian Popular Music*. David & Charles, Newton Abbot.

Poole, H. E. and Krummel, D.W. (1980) Printing and publishing of music. *The New Grove Dictionary of Music and Musicians*, Vol. 15. ed: Stanley Sadie, London.

Poynor, R. (1990) I. *(23) Exhibition/Exposition. Vaughan Oliver*. Espace Graslin, Nantes, CRDC, Nantes. A catalogue.

Poynor, R. (1990) II. Peter Saville's Pentagram for the Nineties. *Blueprint*. November 1990, no. 72 pp. 30–3.

Price, C. M. (1922). *Poster Design. A Critical Study of the Development of the Poster in Continental Europe, England and America*. George W. Bricka, NYC. 1st pub. 1912.

Raynor, H. (1980). *Music in England*. Robert Hale, London.

Redhead, S. (1990). *The End-of-the-Century Party. Youth and Pop towards 2000*. Manchester University Press.

Reid, J. and Savage, J. (1987) *Up they Rise. The Incomplete Works of Jamie Reid*. Faber & Faber, London.

Rimmer, D. (1985). *Like Punk Never Happened. Culture Club and the New Pop*. Faber & Faber, London.

Rogan, J. (1989). *Starmakers and Svengalis. The History of British Pop Management*. Futura Press.

Rose, C. (1988). A Boom of One's Own. *City Limits*, November 3rd, pp. 3–10.

Rueger, C. (1986). *Musical Instruments and their Decoration. Historical Gems of European Culture*. David & Charles, Newton Abbot. (1st pub. 1982, Edition Leipzig.)

Russell, D. (1987) *Popular Music in England. 1840–1914. A Social History*. Music and Society Series. Manchester University Press.

Sandall, R. (1989) I. After the Hits Come the Writs. *The Sunday Times*, October 29th.

Sandall, R. (1990) II. A Backroom Stone Slides into Town. *The Sunday Times*, July 15th.

Sandall, R. (1990) III. Packages without Panache. *The Sunday Times*. April 1st.

Sanjek, R. (1984). *From Print to Plastic. Publishing and Promoting America's Popular Music. (1900–1980)*. Institute for Studies in American Music Monographs. 20. Brooklin Coll., City University of NY., Brooklin.

Sanjek, R. (1988). *American Popular Music and its Business. The First Four Hundred Years*. 3 vols. Oxford University Press, NY.

Searle, A. (1987). *Music Manuscripts*. British Library, London.

Shepard, L. (1969). *John Pitts, Ballad Printer of Seven Dials, London 1765–1844*. London.

Sinclair, J. (1987). *Images Incorporated: Advertising as Industry and Ideology*. Media Debates Series Croom Helm, London.

Smith, G. (1989). The Fine Art of Record Plugging. *The Independent*, March 17th.

Snodin, M. (1983). *George Bickham Junior, Master of the Rococo*. The V&A Album 2.

Spink, I. (1986). *English Song. Dowland to Purcell*. p/b edn. Taplinger Publishing Co., NY.

Taylor, S. (1981). Industrial Manoeuvres in the Art. *The Face*, February.

Thomas, D. (1981). Architecture and Misunderstanding. *Event Magazine*. April 15th–21st.

Tilmouth, M. (1983). *The Beginnings of Provincial Concert Life in England. Music in Eighteenth Century England*. Essays in Memory of Charles Cudworth. Christopher Hogwood and Richard Lucket eds., pp. 1–17.

Tomlinson, A. (1990). *Consumption, Identity and Style. Marketing, Meanings and the Packaging of Pleasure*. Comedia, London & NY.

Tuer, A.W. (1881). *Bartolozzi and his Works*. Field & Tuer, London.

Valpy, N. (1989). Plagiarism in Prints, The Musical Entertainer Affair. *Print Quarterly*, vol. VI no. 1. pp. 54–9.

Van Der Waals, J. (1984). The Print Collection of Sammuel Pepys. *Print Quarterly*, vol. I no. 4. pp. 236–257.

Wale, M. (1972). *Vox Pop. Profiles of the Pop Process*. Harap, London.

Walker, J. A. (1983). *Art in the Age of Mass Media*. Pluto Press, London.

Walker, J. A. (1987). *Cross-Overs. Art into Pop. Pop into Art*. Methuen, London & NY.

Walker, J. A. (1989). *Design History and the History of Design*. Pluto Press, London.

Weber, W. (1975). *Music and the Middle Class. The Social Structure of Concert Life in London, Paris and Vienna*. Croom Helm, London.

Weill, A. (1985). *The Poster. A Worldwide Survey and its History*. Sotheby's Publications London.

White, J. (1990). Season Tickets. *The Independent*, November 30th, p. 17.

Wilk, M. (1973). *Memory Lane 1890–1925. Ragtime, Jazz, Foxtrot and other Popular Music Covers*. Studio International Publications Ltd.

Wozencroft, J. (1988). *The Graphic Language of Neville Brody*. Thames and Hudson, London.

Wulstan, D. (1985). *Tudor Music*. J. M. Dent & Sons Ltd., London.

FURTHER READING

Alexander, J., Consuming Passions - Christ Almighty. *City Limits*, September 15th–22th 1989, pp. 88–89.

Baratelli, J. et al., *IMAGES 33 tours: Couvertures et Pochettes de Disques: Exposition, Cabinet des Estampes*, Geneva, 1981.

Barnard, S., *Tuning-In. Pop on the Radio*. Open University Press, Milton Keynes, 1989.

Benedict, B. and Barton, L., *Phonographis: Contemporary Album Cover Art and Design*. Macmillan. NY, 1977.

Bezzi, P. and Gabici, F., *Il Disco e la sua Copertina: Stile Mode Musicali negli anni '50 e '60*. Ravenna, Essegi, 1988.

Briers, D., *Spin-offs*. Essay accompanying LP record sleeve design exhibition of the same name. Organised by Newport Museum and Art Gallery, 1989.

Brodio, L., *French Opera Posters*. Dover Publications, 1976.

Brunner, F., *A Handbook of Graphic Reproduction Processes*. Verlag Hatje, Stuttgart, 6th revised edn., 1984.

Castle, P. and Bayley, S., *Airflow*. Paper Tiger, 1980.

Clarke, D., *Penguin Encyclopedia of Popular Music*. Penguin Books, 1989.

CLIO Press, *Design*. Modern Art Bibliographical Series. Oxford and Santa Barbara, California, 1984.

Cohn, A. M., *George Cruikshank. A Catalogue Raisonné of the Work Executed During the Years 1806-1877*. The Office of the Bookman's Journal. London, 1924.

Collins, B.R., *Jules Chéret and the Nineteenth Century French Poster*. Ph.D dissertation, Yale University 1980. Dissertation Abstracts International no: 80–35.

Coulson, A. J., *A Bibliography of Design in Britain*, 1851–1970. The Design Council, London, 1979.

Davis, C., Blackwell's Path from Desert Island Discs to Stock Market Risks. *Direction*, January 1987. (Looks at designing for Island Records.)

Dean, R. and Howells, D., *The Album Cover Album* vol. 3. Dragon's World, London, 1984.

Dearling, R. and C. with Rust, B., *The Guinness Book of Recorded Sound*. Guinness Books Enfield, 1984.

Debord, G., *Society of the Spectacle*. Rebel Press/Aim Publications, 1987.

Dieckmann, F., Das Gesicht der Schallplatte. (The Image of the Record), *Bildende Kunst*, pt. 2. February 1979.

EMI. The EMI Collection Catalogue. EMI, London, 1977 (1st pub. 1973).

English, M., *3D Eye–The Posters, Prints & Paintings. of Michael English 1966–1979*. Paper Tiger, Limpsfield, (1st pub. 1979).

Eliot, M., *Rockonomics. The Money Behind the Music*. Omnibus Press, London. 1989.

Errigo, A., and Leaning, S., *The Illustrated History of the Rock Album*. Octopus Books, 1979.

Farren, M., *Get on Down. A Decade of Rock and Roll Posters*. Futura Publications, 1976.

Freidman, M. *et al.*, *Graphic Design in America; a Visual Language History*. Walker Art Center, Minneapolis exhibition catalogue. Harry N. Abrahams Inc., NY, 1989.

Frith, S., *Sound Effects, Youth, Leisure and the Politics of Rock*. Constable, London, 1983.

Frith, S., *Music for Pleasure. Essays in the Sociology of Pop*. Polity Press, 1988.

Frith, S., ed. *Facing the Music. Essays on Pop, Rock and Culture*. Mandarin, London, 1990.

Frith, S., and Goodwin, A., eds. *On Record. Rock Pop, and the Written Word*. Routledge, London. 1990.

Gammond, P., *Scott Joplin and the Ragtime Era*. Abcus/Sphere Books Ltd., 1975.

Garfield, S., *Expensive Habits–The Dark Side of the Music Industry*. Faber & Faber, London, 1986.

Gibson, J., *Getting Noticed. The Musician's Guide to Publicity and Self-Promotion*. From the series The Business of Music. Omnibus Press. 1990. (1st pub. 1988).

Gillett, C., *The Sound of the City*. Souvenir Press, revised edn., London, 1983.

Godbolt, J., *The World of Jazz in Printed Ephemera and Collectibles*. Studio Editions, London, 1990.

Goodwin, A., Sample and Hold. Pop Music in the Digital Age of Reproduction. *Critical Quarterly* 30 (3), 1988. (Reprinted in *On Record*, Frith and Goodwin (1990), pp. 258–273.)

Green, J., *Days in the Life. Voices from the English Underground. 1961–1971*. Heinemann, 1988.

Griffiths, A., *Prints and Printmaking. An Introduction to the History and Techniques*. British Museum Publications Ltd., 1980.

Harris, J. Hyde, S., and Smith, G., *1966 and All That. Design and the Consumer in Britain. 1960-1969*. Trefoil Books, London, 1986.

Heller, S. and Chwast, S., *Graphic Style from Victorian to Post-Modern*. Thames and Hudson, London, 1988.

Hendon, D. W. and Muhs, W. F., Origin and Early Development of Outdoor Advertising in the United States. *Journal of Advertising History*, vol. 9 no. 1, 1986, pp. 7-17. MCB University Press Ltd., Bradford.

Herdeg, W., ed, *Graphis Record Covers: The Evolution of Graphics Reflected in Record Packaging*. Graphis Press, Zürich, 1974.

Hewison, R., *Too Much. Art and Society in the Sixties. 1960-1975*. Methuen, London, 1986.

Hipgnosis, Hardie, G. text: Thorgerson, S., *The Work of Hipgnosis. Walk Away René*, Limpsfield, Dragon's World, 1989.

Hudson, G., Printed Ephemera and Design History. *Art Libraries Journal*, vol. 6 pt. 1, Spring 1981, pp. 20–32.

i-D Magazine. *A Decade of i-Deas. The Encyclopedia of the '80s*. Compiled and produced by i-D Magazine, London, 1990.

Jasen, D. A., *Tin Pan Alley. The Composers, the Songs, the Performers and their Times*. Omnibus Press. 1990. (1st pub. 1988).

Kidson, F., *British Music Publishers, Printers and Engravers etc*. W. E. Hill and Sons, London, c.1900.

King, A. H., *A Wealth of Music in the Collections of The British Library (Reference Division) and The British Museum*. A guide to the catalogues. London, 1983.

Krummel, D. W. and Sadie, S. *Music Printing and Publishing*. The New Grove Handbooks in Music. Macmillan Press, London, 1990

Lambert, S., *The Image Multiplied. Five Centuries of Printed Reproductions of Paintings and Drawings*. Trefoil Publications, London, 1987.

Makower, J., *Woodstock, The Oral History*. Sidgwick and Jackson, 1989.

Matthaias, F., Prelude to Profit. *Creative Review*, March 1989, pp. 41–2. [On the LCO].

McDermott, C., *Street Style. British Design in the '80s*. The Design Council, London, 1987.

McInnes, C., *Sweet Saturday Night. Pop Song. 1840–1920*. MacGibbon & Kee, London, 1967.

Melly, G., *Revolt into Style*, Allen Lane, London, 1970.

Musée Des Arts Decoratifs, *L'Affiche Anglaise: Les Années 90*. Paris, 1972.

Neal, C., *Tape Delay*. SAF (Publishing) Ltd., Harrow, 1987.

Prato, P., Musical Kitsch: Close Encounters Between Pops and Classics. In Cutler, C. (1985).

Rachlin, H., *The Encyclopedia of the Music Business*. Harper and Row, NY, 1981.

Reynolds, S. *Blissed Out. The Raptures of Rock*. Serpent's Tail, 1990.

Riordan, J., *Making it in the New Music Business*. From the series The Business of Music, Omnibus Press, 1988, esp. pp. 150–211.

Rüegg R., *Basic Typography: Design with Letters*. ABC–

Verlag Zürich, 1989.

Schauer, L. *et al.*, Schallplattenhüllen: Funktion und Bildwelten. Berlin, GFR. *Neur Berliner Kunstverein*, April 29th–May 25th 1978.

Schmitz, M. *Album Cover Geschichte und Ästhetik einer Schallplattenverpackung in den USA nach 1940: Designer–Stile–Inhalte*. (With interviews in English). Scaneg, Munich, 1987.

Scott, D., *The Singing Bourgeois. Songs of the Victorian Drawing Room and Parlour*. From the series Popular Music in Britain. Open University Press, Milton Keynes, 1989.

Searle, A., *Haydn and England*. British Library, London, 1989.

Shepard, L., *The Broadside Ballad. The Development of the Street Ballad from Traditional Song to Popular Newspapers*. Legacy Books, Hatboro, PA, USA, 1978.

Smith, C. S., *Broadsides and their Music in Colonial America. Music in Colonial Massachusetts*, I. Music in Public Places. Conference Paper, The Colonial Society of Massachusetts, Boston, 1980, pp, 157–367.

Supicić, I., *Music in Society: A Guide to the Sociology of Music*. Sociology of Music no.4, Pendragon Press, Stuyvesant, NY, 1987.

Thames and Hudson, *Graphic Designers in Europe*, vol. 1. Jan Lenica, Jean-Michel Folon, Josef Müller-Brockmann, Dick Elfers. London, 1971.

Thorgerson, S. and Dean, R., *The Album Cover Album*. Limpsfield, Dragon's World, 1977.

Thorgerson, S., Dean, R. and Howells, D., *The Album Cover Album*. vol. 2. Paper Tiger, London, c.1982.

Thorgerson, S., *Classic Album Covers of the '60s*. Paper Tiger London, 1989.

Wacholtz, L. E. *Inside Country Music*. Billboard Publications Inc., 1986.

Waites, A., and Hunter, R., *The Illustrated Victorian Songbook*. Michael Joseph, London, 1984.

Walker, C. G., ed. *The Great Poster trip. Art Eureka*. Coyne and Blanchard, Inc., 1968.

Wedgbury, D., A Feel for the Classics. *Illustrators*, no. 61, March 1988. (Looks at Decca Records and classical sleeve design).

Weill, A., *100 Years of Posters of the Folies-Bergère and Music Halls of Paris*, NY Images Graphiques, 1977.

Whitely, N. W. *Pop Designs, Modernism to Mod*. The Design Council, London, 1987.

Wild, N., *Les Arts du Spectacle en France: Affiches Illustrées 1850-1960*. Bibliothèque Nationale, 1976.

INDEX

PICTURE CREDITS